I DIDN'T SEE THAT COMING... BUT HE DID!

I Didn't See That Coming… But He Did!
Copyright © 2023 by Steven G. Casado

Published in the United States of America
ISBN   Paperback: 979-8-89091-318-0
ISBN   eBook: 979-8-89091-319-7

All rights reserved. No part of this publication may be reproduced, stored in a retrieval system or transmitted in any way by any means, electronic, mechanical, photocopy, recording or otherwise without the prior permission of the author except as provided by USA copyright law.

The opinions expressed by the author are not necessarily those of ReadersMagnet, LLC.

ReadersMagnet, LLC
10620 Treena Street, Suite 230 | San Diego, California, 92131 USA
1.619. 354. 2643 | www.readersmagnet.com

Book design copyright © 2023 by ReadersMagnet, LLC. All rights reserved.

Cover design by Ericka Obando
Interior design by Daniel Lopez

I DIDN'T SEE THAT COMING... BUT HE DID!

Steven G. Casado

ReadersMagnet, LLC

DEDICATION

This book was written to inspire those who have walked a similar path or know a person or people who have suffered or are suffering in the same manner as I have encountered. This book was created to provide facts in different areas of my life and for therapeutic purposes as a reminder of where I was and where I needed to be to become a better person. This book was not intended for character assassination. I have forgiven all parties for their wronging and am comfortable expressing these events in my life. It's a reminder of the weakness my family and I relinquished and a reminder of the strength we have gained through faith in Jesus Christ. To look back and see how far we have traveled is remarkable and everybody has a story, including you! Diabetes and abandonment issues were a war, and destroyed me physically, while emotional scars were developing. I needed hope! If you are weak in any manner, find faith through Christ and allow yourself to go under construction because, in the end, this book was written to show that anything is possible with *God*!

ACKNOWLEDGMENT

I would like to first acknowledge both my parents for becoming the strong individuals that they are, and without them, I literally would not be alive. I love my dad for many reasons, but one specific is that he allowed God to break the generational curse of drugs and alcohol. My life and this book would be entirely different without you playing the role you and Mom did, and although it took me a very long time to realize it, I was blessed to go through all I encountered because now I have a story to tell. I acknowledge it, appreciate it, and thank you both for loving me!

The next group I would like to acknowledge are my best friends, who I consider family, Michael Silva, Jaclyn Spaccarelli, and Adam Rosenthal. Thank you for always inspiring me because, in three different timelines, you all told me that I should write a book one day. It wasn't a matter of if but when, and the three of you kept me encouraged while I was constructing this manuscript, and I am most appreciative of how you've impacted my life and never left my side.

I would like to show gratitude towards my sister in Christ, Bailey O'Brien, for showing the most support for all the years I was working on this project. You always showed that you cared about my well-being in every aspect of my health, including spiritual. What you displayed to me was the love of God which motivated me to be more Christ-like. You have impacted my life in a great manner, and I'm honored to call you a friend.

I would like to show my appreciation to Joe Urbanowicz, one of the godly men at the First Baptist church who held on to me when nobody else was around. Joe explained to me what "humility" was all about, and although it took me years to learn and grow with it, the seed was planted, and I am forever grateful to him for never leaving me behind. Joe has known me for over two decades and has been one of the greatest instruments that God could bless me with for guidance and to lead others towards the Truth.

The final person that I would like to acknowledge is Edward Klopper. During a time when guidance was needed, you prevailed and provided it to me. You spoke to me in a method that was so captivating with details that you allowed learning to become a lot of fun. You taught me how to speak well and provided confidence that launched me to be the man I am today, and I can't thank you enough for how you blessed me but thank you again!

TABLE OF CONTENTS

Dedication v
Acknowledgment vii
Preface xiii

Chapter 1: The Beginning...1
Chapter 2: A Field of Sadness 9
Chapter 3: Imprisoned By Torment...............................23
Chapter 4: Freshman/Sophomore Years........................35
Chapter 5: Many Transitions 53
Chapter 6: What I Wanted...64
Chapter 7: Foolishly Entrapped To Incarceration.................89
Chapter 8: Roller Coaster Ride 102
Chapter 9: What Do I Do Now?..................................119
Chapter 10: Chaotic Conundrum................................130
Chapter 11: Rock Bottom To Willpower......................144
Chapter 12: My Testimony: Lost & Found Faith 165
Chapter 13: Final Words 171

About The Author 175

PREFACE

The story I am about to tell you is based on life events that fashioned me into the man I am today! There were many avenues that were ventured in my rise, and many of those paths were not an easy trail to follow, especially without the proper council. Life threw many hindrances, and it swallowed me without remorse when making unwise decisions. You might find some situations familiar or know someone that might be experiencing the same hurt as I. Sibling rivalry, diabetes, abuse, loneliness, therapy, drug abuse, relationship choices, work ethics, and faith are roads I've meandered through, and hope you can pick up something through my journey. I had to make a choice, either trust God or myself and when He stepped in, it was amazing to see the power of the best reinforcement. This book was not created for a specific demographic but may spark an interest to those who encountered any of the previously mentioned categories. I hope you enjoy my life story because I went through hell, diabetes broke me but God assembled me back together!

CHAPTER 1

THE BEGINNING

I, Steven G. Casado, am a summer baby, born in the city of *Manhattan* and arrived in this world on August 18th, 1985, on a Sunday morning. My mother not only had a C-Section at six and a half months, but she was blessed with twins, and Desiree was born two minutes after me. *"Desiree"* is a French moniker that means *"the desired one,"* and the name *"Steven"* is an American and Greek moniker that means *"crown and victorious."* It has been acknowledged that men with this name have a deep inner desire to use their leadership abilities and personal independence. They are capable, charismatic leaders who often successfully undertake large activities. They value truth, justice, and discipline and may be quick-tempered with those who are not aligned in their manner.

If they fail to develop their potential, they may become impractical and even rigid.

My family consists of five members, as I have an older brother. It was expressed to me that at birth, I could fit in the palm of the hand of the doctor. Desiree was the healthier baby, and I was at risk of not making it, but even as an infant, I fought to survive! I was premature and was diagnosed with asthma and had to remain in the hospital for some additional time. Based on my performances in the incubator, I was quite flexible, which had my parents in questionable shock but in an optimistic fashion based on what had been expressed to me. The expedition of growing up was not elementary, and it took many years of wisdom to see why I had experienced continuous trials. It's unfortunate that I recall more negative circumstances than constructive ones, but that's because those were emotionally charged events and I was often disappointed and didn't know how to rub this off. I felt that I was a problem child and believed this to be true because I was always getting in trouble and was afraid of disappointing my parents based on my poor choice of actions.

It was not easy growing up, and my mind created an emotional barrier based on a lack of love for me in comparison to what my sister received. After all, she is the *"desired one."* My parents may disagree, but the feeling was real, and it hurt me very much, and I did not enjoy the sting it presented. I recall a conversation with Desiree regarding things that occurred while she was not home, and she remarked, *"Stop lying!"* If you know me, you'll know that professing me a liar will darken my happiness, especially if I'm trying to make a point! She mentioned, *"We used to go to the park all the time,"* and *"That never happened!"* She was often doing auditions and or filming something, so how can one who is not present have a say of any kind about what transpired outside of their observation and claim *"that never happened"*? It wasn't like it was written down on paper to show what occurred around the house, like a diary or the Bible, but if Desiree were to tell you her lifestyle growing up, her story would be completely different from mine!

I wasn't exactly the easiest son or brother to have around, either. I mean, one afternoon Desiree and I had a disagreement about a movie we were watching on the television, and I knew for a fact that for a couple of minutes, the movie was in reverse, like looking in a mirror, and when she disagreed and called me a liar, I saw red, and I bit her leg just because of her remark, yet I was vocalizing a true statement. I was so exasperated that I left my teeth marks on her leg. There was no denying my harm, and after my sister screamed, I thought I positioned myself in some deep waters and would get the tail-whooping of my life! My grandmother then asked, *"Nene, you bit her leg? I see your teeth marks!"* I felt guilt but revealed little emotion, so I paid little mind to it. I'm glad to say that I do not remember the consequences, but if I were Desiree, I would've knocked Steven out with my foot, knee, or fist, boom!

I mean, how could a kid, not even in double digits in age, be so triggered to rage? Rumor has it that you can become a product of your environment! My first word as a baby was *"No,"* so that had me thinking about what was articulated towards me for that to be my first word. I did not know whether this was common or rare for babies, but I observed this as negative. The public-school kids were no aid to me, as many were bullies! Desiree and I are very dissimilar regarding our choice of friends, the movies or television shows we watch, the music we listen to, or even the food we enjoy. Desiree even writes with her right hand, whereas I'm a lefty like my dad. If there is one thing that Desiree and I can agree on, it's that we do not care for sports at all! It's just not our thing. The way I see it, if we were not related, we wouldn't even be friends or speak to each other. That might sound rude, but it's agreeable. A lot of people enter this world alone, but I was fortunate to have company, and although I may not say it, there is love for my sister somewhere within me. I mean, I'm sure being a parent for the first time isn't easy for anyone, am I wrong? If Michael and I were ever home together, I usually saw him when wrestling was broadcasted on the television or when he was playing on the Sega Genesis or Nintendo. I would try to assemble the consoles when Michael wasn't around because sometimes, he would disconnect them, and when he would play, I was lucky if he allowed me to even observe his gameplay because if this was not possible, the words *"Get Out"* were sure to be waiting for me to receive. I mean, I don't really recall being with Michael as much as I would have liked, so I often felt alone, and I'm sure I didn't see Michael regularly at home because he didn't want to be there!

When I felt the brotherly bond when it presented itself, it was great to experience the moment because brotherly guidance was what I needed. I was walking with Michael one day in the streets of *The Bronx* when these two kids were playing football on the sidewalk, and a football flew over one kid's head and was headed towards my direction. I caught the ball, and one youngster said, *"Wow, this little kid caught it!"* Michael and I proceeded with our walk, and I tossed the football back with an extended smile on my face. Since sports is not an enjoyment of mine; to catch the ball and hear Michael say, *"Yeah, that's my brother,"* was a gratifying moment for me. One kid responded to his buddy, *"It would've been funny if it hit him."* As Michael and I walked, he said to this young teen, *"You're lucky it didn't hit my brother!"* Once this was stated, Michael extended his right arm over my right shoulder, and I thought this was the first time my brother showed me support. Perhaps there was another instance when he asked me to trade his *"Beavis and Butthead"* video game for *"MK 2"* with a friend from school, and since I saw Michael with a rare smile after doing this task for him, I knew he was proud of my effort.

However, there was an evening when brotherly conflict would occur because I was in our room while he was gaming, and when he lost in the video game he was playing, I was blamed for it and told, *"Get out!"* which made my blood boil! Once Michael vacated the room, I would eventually walk in, climb to the top bunk, go underneath a thin sheet, and softly begin singing *"This little piggy..."*

as a scapegoat for what would happen next. When I got to my middle finger, boy, did that finger go up, and when Michael lifted the sheet, there I was, flipping him the bird! I got yanked down, became frantic, and was brought to my mother, who was in the hallway. I denied my actions to her and went about my evening. Michael blamed the public school for my actions, and although he was correct, this was the common language of the streets that I observed through many people, including students.

My mom worked in the finance department for a Japanese bank and worked with numbers daily, transferring millions through transactions, looking for and fixing errors which is probably why I love math and puzzles. She was also a fierce woman, but most kids love being around their mom, correct? I was always told by my Uncles, Aunts, and Dad that Mom was the rough one out of the five children God blessed for my grandmother. I'm not sure what it's like to have a child, let alone twins like my mom or five children like my grandmother, but I could imagine it wasn't easy for either of them! I remember scanning outside my bedroom window, waiting for the train to arrive at around 5 pm at the *East 180*th train station, and once I saw that train, I knew mom would be home within twenty-five minutes, which brought me a sense of joy unless I had a bad report card. I recall an early afternoon when my Dad and I had a disagreement about something foolish, so I called mom frantic, trying to explain what was happening, not realizing that my father was listening right outside his bedroom door. He approached me with this disgusted look, and I felt robbed because it was his drunk words against my words, and I knew that I was about to pay his tab in the sense of who would pay for it! The phone was snatched from my hand. I stomped my feet and walked towards the window and felt embraced by darkness from this negative energy inside my mind. Since he had been drinking, this wasn't going to work well in my favor! I won't clarify what transpired after that scene, but I remember running out of my parent's room, scurrying towards mine, and by the end of this altercation, I slept a night of tears underneath the bunk bed.

Desiree stated to me the following morning, *"Dad was really sorry,"* as she placed her right hand over my left shoulder. When you feel frightened about every move you make, all you want to do is be around those that make you feel safe. My mother was the one who fit that criterion at home until I made her upset! I am certain that every parent living, past, present and or future has and will encounter a dilemma with their children. As a child, my mother was my hero because if I were ill, she'd be there! If I had too much homework, she'd tell me the answers to questions I did not know if it was past my bedtime. If I were awfully exhausted in the morning prior to attending school, she'd dress me while I was still sleeping. Mom took Desiree and me to *"Ground Round"* for a great family lunch and IHop on Wednesdays because children ate for free this day of the week! Mom was being a mom and was there unconditionally, and nobody can take that away from her!

Dad was a loss prevention manager and the artiste of the family! I've seen him make some pretty awesome things out of nothing. This is regarding science projects, forming a meal, home improvement, whatever! I remember my dad, in 1992, making me a science project that was the arm of a human body and how it operates with the triceps and bicep muscles. My father used two empty paper towel rolls and small balloons. If you place your arm at a 45-degree angle, like the shape of an "L," where your triceps and bicep muscles are located, those are the balloons. I was awarded 2nd place, and I was thrilled because it was the *State Science Fair*! My father is a handyman but was also that guy you did not want to have a conflict with because, just like my mother, he, too, was fierce! I recall my father inquiring one afternoon who my friends were, so I hung my head, stated a few names, felt interrogated and felt like there was a breach to my life that I wanted in secrecy. My dad then looked at Michael and instructed him to inform me who my friends were, and Michael uttered with intensity, *"We are your friends!"* A friend is a person one knows and has a mutual bond with, but I didn't feel I had friends at my residence. The difference between my parents through my lenses was that my dad was an alcoholic, and my mom was a cigarette smoker, but one thing they always did was provide for their kids.

CHAPTER 2

A FIELD OF SADNESS

Growing up with a twin sister who I felt was the golden child allowed me to feel like I had to be bold because I didn't want to be known as this angry kid who was repetitively encountering unfair scenarios. I'm not saying anything destructive about my family, but can anyone explain the image of a *"normal"* family? Before anybody can be old and wise, they are first young and foolish, and I was a child, so I knew where I categorized myself. I didn't ask to be how I was, but how I was, was not how I wanted to be, and I was young and clueless on how to resolve *"tough"* situations due to lack of experience since I was just a kid. I do recall my dad loving to record homemade videos with my sister and me, and most of the time, it was fun, except for this one day that will never escape my memory.

My dad instructed my sister and me on what to do so the video looked fluent and not rehearsed, even though it was staged. Down our hallway were two bedrooms on the left-hand side, first my parents' room, then the room shared between their three kids; the immediate left of our bedroom was the bathroom. Dad positioned the camera at the base of the hallway, and Desiree and I were in our parent's room. I was the first one to leave, make a left and proceed toward the restroom. When I walked into the bathroom and up my step stool, I looked at the mirror; Dad said, *"Cut,"* and he walked from down the hall and resumed the video once positioned in the corner of the bathroom. The objective was to shave with a bladeless razor and not look at the camera, but of course, I messed up! I didn't know what to do since there was hardly any shaving cream on my face, and I was fearful of messing up. I looked over my right shoulder towards the camera to ask, *"Now what?"* Once this occurred, I caught a hard smack to the face with dad's left hand for not following directions. I didn't see that coming!

This was supposed to be fun but became miserable for me. My dad then went back towards the end of the hall to resume the recording, and if you were to look at that VHS tape today, when my dad resumed the recording, my eyes were flooded with tears as I walked back into my parents' room with my head hung. Desiree saw me and questioned, *"What happened?"* I replied, *"Whatever you do, don't look at the camera!"* Desiree advanced to the bathroom while I remained in the room, and as my face fell, rage and resentment formed within because I felt hopeless. The emotional rise of brokenness began its development, and I thought while weeping, *"I'll never be good enough for anything,"* and wiped my eyes quickly. It was a matter of minutes before I had to leave the room for my dad to resume the video, and I did not want to portray myself as a wimp.

I was around six years of age and already had a negative attitude about existing! I was molded with soft tissue and unfortunately at times was attacked with the heavy weight of anger from my parents. I never saw Desiree get disciplined, and the punishments I received from my mother made me infuriated because I already had a not-so-great relationship with my dad. Since I feared the anger of both my parents, my mind formed some sort of barrier, often making me feel like I was walking on eggshells. I just wanted to be at grandma's because in her apartment there were no eggshells.

I recall having a penmanship assignment, and as my dad is the creative one, he would be the person helping me with this writing assignment, as this made sense since we both write with our left hand. My handwriting was terrible, and I remember my father yelling at me because my penmanship was not appealing at all! My dad's handwriting looks like it's typed, and he wanted mine to be at least legible and between the lines which made sense. I went to school the next day and saw a student's handwriting and thought, *"That's what dad wants it to look like, okay!"* I learned from this student how to improve my penmanship to prevent my dad from shouting at me. The next time he saw my handwriting, he was very impressed, which made me feel triumphant to see him jubilant of me.

Desiree and I were often at grandma's apartment, and one afternoon, my cousin Jessica was over and took us both to the park, and it was pleasant until an emergency occurred! There was a unique slide that I wanted to attend and mimic what I saw others doing. The slide was actually rolling pins, and on the horizontal section, I saw kids running on it to make the rolling pins move faster, so others dropped quickly to the bottom. I did it for a little while, but the pins were rolling too fast, and I could not keep up and fell on my face and down the slide. Jessica freaked out because not only was my mouth all bloody, but I cracked my front tooth as well and looked like Lloyd from *"Dumb and Dumber."* I told my cousin I'd be fine, but you know that comment couldn't keep me bound in the park. When I looked in the mirror, I was embarrassed, but it didn't bother me in the sense that I didn't smile much, so not many people were going to see my broken tooth until I spoke. As the school year was coming to an end, we had to take photos for the yearbook, and now I became annoyed with frustration. Within me was a broken spirit hiding behind a broken smile inside this breaking vessel of a body. It was bad enough that all eyes were on me for being so short, and now this chipped tooth would only give others more of a reason to pick on me. Great!

The summertime was here, and it was expected to be great. I remember going to the planetarium for the first time. It was an amazing experience to view such a sight because I had no knowledge of outer space or meteors until this point, which was a transcending joy for me! The following month, I recall my mother telling my sister and me that our great-grandfather had died. I distinctly remember questioning mom, *"I thought everybody lived forever?"* So, eight days prior to my birthday, great grandpa was not going to be present. I didn't know how to respond to such news, but great grandpa was a *"man's man,"* according to my dad. My father also stated that great grandpa traveled the world, spoke well, and grew up in an era where men were real men! I didn't understand much of Papi Wello's speech because his primary language was Spanish, and I was not raised learning this tongue, but he did make me laugh even though I didn't understand most of his speech, with or without his teeth. The humility of an elderly person can grant much joy when you know how to receive them.

Do you remember being a child and craving something so badly you would make a scene without negative intentions but knew you just messed up and angered your parents? I remember my mother saying one day in *Toys" R" Us* to me, *"You're embarrassing me! You want me to give you a reason to cry?" Now this was a very common question within the streets of The Bronx and Hispanic kids, so I know I wasn't the only one who heard this rhetorical question.* I understood why my mother questioned what she asked but saying it with a different tone would've made a bigger difference in how the message would have been received. Actually, never mind, I take that back because, in this case, a different tone would make no difference since it's a negative question! I don't recall receiving many words of affirmation, which probably could have helped mold me in many situations. *"A gentle answer turns away wrath, but a harsh word stirs up anger."* (Proverbs 15:1)

Michael wasn't exactly the pleasantest brother growing up, and I felt like I had nothing in common with Desiree except for DNA. Feeling as if there was a measure of a standard that I could never reach, I perceived myself as the black sheep of the family and often strode with an indignant look upon my face, which became exhausting, and there is a cause and effect in all scenarios! I have another cousin Jazmin, who took Desiree and me to the park for a while one morning, and when we returned to Grandma's apartment, I thought it would be okay to stand clear of everyone and sit in Jazmin's closet. Mom grew frantic, questioning Jazmin where I was last seen, and she stated that she had come up with both Desiree and me. I didn't realize how much time was passing and eventually saw an arm reach in the closet in search of me, but I was too comfortable and, for a hot minute, acknowledged that mom would indeed care if I went missing. What felt like over an hour had gone by quickly, and she made a second attempt to search in the closet, and this time, she found me! I was escorted out by her grabbing my leg and then pulling my ear while yelling at me for deliberately hiding and then whooped my ass! I guess I can't blame her, but now I really wanted to run away, and that angry, broken face summoned itself upon me, and all I wanted was a sense of freedom. So much for this Summer being great because it's not going well whatsoever! I need to shape up!

Walking with mom and Desiree through the borough, I recall glancing at a dojo not too far from the library when I requested my mother about joining karate, but the response received was *"You can't do that and no!"* which are not words of encouragement! I'm sure there was a concern for my health if people were hitting me; punches or kicks and I could get seriously hurt, so logically, I get it, and I was pushed to seek psychological help instead, which provided an abundance of frustration at first because I really wanted to partake in karate to channel my aggression! If I wanted something but was told *"No,"* I might whine about it, and if I did, there was a good probability of me getting disciplined by either parent, so I knew to remain silent about the self-defense classes and hid my feelings. We sought out therapy sessions, and in one of those meetings, Michael and my mother were with me while Desiree and dad remained in the waiting room!

At this moment, Michael was to pretend he was a stranger who snuck up on me, pinning my elbows to my ribcage with his arms cuffed around my left and right shoulder. Although I saw how I would escape in my mind, in reality, I acted helpless because if I had fashioned my thoughts into existence, I probably would have looked like a menace, but hence why I wanted to do karate! Within the next month, I was prescribed medication, and although I did not want this drug, I was told that its purpose was for my stability.

As usual, Desiree and I had a disagreement, and I articulated in a calm manner that I wanted to react angrily but was utterly weary of fighting. I always wanted the last word, so when Desiree replied, *"Good, the medicine is working!"* I was in denial about this drug having progress on me, so I countered, *"Shut up!"* and strapped on the face of disappointment. I was my own worst enemy and was smothered with jealousy towards my sister because Desiree was granted two opportunities of enjoyment, doing ballet and tap dancing, whereas I was simply denied from partaking in karate! I'll get over it! Tick-Tock!

My dad isn't a master in martial arts, but man, did he know a thing or two about black belts. I was afraid of getting whooped by my dad and or getting my ear pulled by my mom, who has no idea how elevating my body from my ear to the point where I was on my tip toes is wrong! I always heard crackling and have been titled an elf by some students because my ear would appear stretched. Is this a Steven problem or a family issue? Could I really have been that terrible of a child? Maybe, and being short-statured enabled the bullying to develop rapidly at school. This was another reason why I wanted to take karate; I did not know how to defend myself! I needed a way to channel my aggression and focus on positive teachings instead of relying on my feelings, which misguided me all the time. I continued seeing the psychoanalyst and eventually thought how delightful it was to speak with somebody outside my family since she could break down my mental barriers without biases.

It would be confirmed that I was a smart bitter child, diagnosed with A.D.D., taking Ritalin and began to open up, noticing a diminutive difference within myself which was important and somewhere down the line I was eventually prescribed Zoloft. Ritalin was provided to me because I was told that this medication stimulates the mind and body and can calm down adults and children. When I was prescribed Zoloft, it was either for "Major Depressive Disorder" (MDD) or "Social Anxiety Disorder" (SAD) but if I wanted to see a change, I needed to make a change! The therapy sessions occurred for some years but only assisted me for as long as I wanted the help. My therapist also informed me to keep in mind that my parents are a result of their rise up, which may not have been so easy for them! I mean, what made dad turn to drink, and why was mom rough with discipline? Did they love their children? They took care of us, so yes, they absolutely do, but just like anybody walking this earth, none of us are perfect.

I remember the Spring of 1996 when my mother picked up Desiree and me from school and informed us of the passing of our uncle Billy. This man had a personality that always brought a smile to anyone's face. He was the joker of the family and was one of the best! When my mother explained the situation, another darkened expression developed upon yours truly, and I stated, *"That's not funny!"* I mentioned this because if this news were to be true, my uncle would have met his demise on his favorite day, April Fools. Cancer stole my uncle away from the family, and that was a hard pill to swallow because the smiles he permitted me to have would be no more.

The school year was going to end in a couple of months, and not only did I graduate from the 5th grade, but I was graduating to the 6-F class. I recall walking down the stairs with my classmates in a panic as I opened up my report card, and then my pupils expanded; I froze and said to my friend, *"My parents are going to kill me! I failed without failing!"* My friend Yazzy responded, *"You still passed. Cheer up!"* As we proceeded to exit the school grounds, I was more afraid with every step I took, and my mental barrier was forming, fearing for the worst! My dad was coming to pick up my sister and me, and I was frightened, not of my dad but of my mother this time! When I arrived home, my mother said, *"Let me see your 4th quarter report card."* I handed over my final progress report, and after glancing at it she remarked, "Good, you passed!" A negative tone was not expressed when she articulated this, so there was an uplifting relief in my heart when I heard those words. Overanalyzing the situation only created fear of the unknown! Who could blame a kid for being nervous from being a "C" student to declining to an "F" student? My parents weren't exactly the tranquil type, so I couldn't help but be concerned about my mother's reaction to the report card, but it was nice to be at ease.

I often allowed myself to feel that *"panic"* and *"fear"* were my only friends at home. There are good and bad times in all situations, but not everything was so terrible with my dad because there were two things that allowed me to gain respect for him outside of our residence. The first was seeing my dad in work mode on the security footage of his job. There was a *10-31* in motion, a *"Crime in Progress,"* where a thief was caught trying to vacate the premises with stolen goods. When my dad apprehended the criminal, the shoplifter tried to flee, but then my dad flipped him on a rack of CDs and slapped on the handcuffs. Seeing my dad in this video made me proud to have him as my father. The second situation that allowed me to gain additional respect for him was when we attended *Nathan's* on *Central Avenue* in *Yonkers*, where we'd eat dinner, followed by entering the arcade.

I observed dad mastering the claw machine very well, and his eye coordination was so on point that his performance brought a small crowd to form behind him and observe his mastery. A young kid even questioned his parents if they could give my dad money to grab these husky stuffed animals, but by the end of this evening, we walked out with over a dozen of them! Seeing this assemblage of people so amazed by the talent he performed on the claw machine, my dad was like the MVP, and I was in awe on this night. When we arrived home, we had a lot of laughs watching *Ren & Stimpy* as always! For the record, our fishing trips were always an awesome experience as well. The most influential role model in a kid's life is the parent of the same-sex, and I needed that strong leadership.

On a particular Saturday during the Summer, my dad brought me to his job, but not because it was *"Bring your kid to work day,"* but because there was a celebrity wrestler that was making an appearance for an autograph signing! When I saw *"The Undertaker"* enter the loss prevention backroom, I was a deer in headlights because I had never stood so close to a Goliath. Once the autograph signing concluded, Michael, dad, and I were given tickets to go to *Madison Square Garden* to see a "House Show" which is an event that doesn't appear on television. This surprise put the feather in the cap on that day and I was thrilled!

There's a saying, *"There's no place like home,"* but there was surely no place like Grandma's residence because there was always a reason to smile! *Blockbuster* was within walking distance, as was the pizzeria and park, so it was a win-win all the time. On many occasions, Desiree and I would take the bus with grandma or our aunt Mady to travel to the *Whitestone Cinema*, which was an adventurous treat! I also relished going to Grandma's doctor appointments because that meant taking a trip to *Manhattan!* Grandma is a devoted catholic, and when she would attend church retreats, Desiree and I would tag along, and although it was often fun, if you were trying to talk to me about God instead of letting me enjoy the atmosphere, I was not willing to pay attention because my Gameboy was more appealing at this age. I may have heard words projected, but I was not quick to listen. On another note, when it came to eating food by the most experienced woman in the family, it was like being in heaven, yet there is no comparison.

1 Peter 3:8 says, *"Finally, all of you, be like-minded, be sympathetic, love one another, be compassionate and humble."* I can see h ow and what my grandmother wanted to represent. She knows that Jesus is God, Jesus is Love itself and that He loves me! That was the message she wanted to elaborate on, and I was grateful because all I wanted was to feel treasured! My aunt Mady and Cousin Jazmin were the icings on the cake because they lived in the projects with Grandma. I recall laying on Jazmin's bed watching *"Cartoon Network"* and asking Desiree to get me orange juice. She thought I was being lazy, which was understandable, and declined my request, so about twenty or so minutes later, I said inside my head with an angry tone that I would just get it myself. I got close but not close enough before collapsing on the ground. Jazmin ran to me after she heard something in the hallway dropping hard, which was me. She picked me up, placed me on the bed, and someone provided me with juice. I had never experienced feeling so feeble before, and this was the first run of this type of episode. Desiree expressed regret moments later for not believing me as she placed her hand on my shoulder and apologized. Desiree is very humble, whereas I can't say the same about me at our age.

The first week of August of 1996 was enjoyable as Grandma blessed Desiree and me with outdoor ventures to the park, which had water sprinklers as a bonus, got some Italian ice and eventually, lunch would be arranged as always. Grandma has type 2 diabetes and saw the symptoms of constant thirst and frequent urination within me, which was not a good sign. She checked my blood sugar, which recorded my glucose at 550. No rejoicing would arise from this disappointing news, and it often seemed like dissatisfaction was often gnawing at me. The average blood-sugar ranges between 80 and 120, and mine was 550, so if you compare what the numbers should be versus where it was, you can imagine that I'm about to slip into *a field of sadness*. When she said, *"Ne-ne, you have diabetes,"* I closed my eyes, my face fell, and time froze. As usual, I became an emotional wreck, and everything went blank! I ran from the dining room table to the bathroom with flooded eyes and slowly converted from emotional hurt into aggressive anger! Wondering why I was dealt so many terrible cards, I grew more jealous of Desiree because now I had another restriction in my life, little to no sugar in my diet. My heart of flesh now wanted to become a heart of stone! When I couldn't think of any reason to be jovial, negative emotions, unfortunately, conquered my movements and clouded my judgment!

CHAPTER 3

IMPRISONED BY TORMENT

When I was admitted to *Montefiore Hospital* for two weeks the following day, it happened to turn out to be delightful! My aunt Mady brought the VHS tape of *The Lost World*, and the hospital provided the Sega Genesis and Super Nintendo. I felt excited to be around all my family and even recall my dad elaborating to me, *"I will never lay another hand on you again!"* When disciplinary actions were taken to keep me in line, it was required because I chose not to listen. Looking at his body language with his elbows on his knees, arms extended out, and hands folded, he seemed sincere, but I didn't know what to believe. This was the first promise I remember Dad making to me, and I can proudly say that he kept his word! There was suddenly a sign of hope! My father knew his son was ill, and he looked devastated by this news.

When he made this oath, I thought that perhaps it might be okay having diabetes after all because God took a disease, bestowed me with its company, and now Dad disabled himself from hitting me if I chose to act out! I understood that pricking my fingers and taking insulin multiple times a day would be a part of my daily routine to remain healthy, but I acknowledged this as negative because of the literal sting it presented to my fingertips and injection sites. The more I thought about it, the more I resented diabetes because I had to celebrate my birthday with a sugar-free cake which was torment within itself! Who wants that? Not me, but I had to rise up and understood that this was my role, and felt I had to prove something! If sin didn't enter the world, I wouldn't have diabetes, but it did, and I do!

I had to prove that I was a survivor; after all, I had been fighting for survival since birth! When I was in the hospital and felt the support from my family, I didn't feel so alienated anymore. Every day God gives us many reasons to rejoice, and the rest is simply up to us! My attitude and lifestyle had to change, but I did not want to relinquish sugar for diet sweeteners! A diet "anything" was not pleasant to my taste buds, and considering I was only fifty-five pounds, it didn't make sense to me why I should consume anything diet. It hurt to witness Desiree enjoy her cake and ice cream while I bogusly enjoyed mine! The school was going to start in approximately two weeks, and I wasn't sure how this would work out. I was always a "C" student since the first grade. I was in classes 1-C, 2-C, 3-C,

4-C, and 5-C! Mathematics was my forte; numbers are collectively used daily, so it was easy to assemble numbers in an arrangement that made it into a game. I mean, even a broken clock is correct twice a day, and that's with no effort. Numbers fascinate me, and I was nominated as the *"Math Magician"* as opposed to *"mathematician"* from first grade through fifth by the teachers and the votes of the students. I use numbers to remember events, timelines, telephone numbers and simple things like counting money, so since this is used daily, I wanted to know more, and that credit goes to Mom for me having this trait.

Entering the 6th grade with this disease was not going to be easy because I didn't really comprehend diabetes to its fullest. A side effect of elevated glucose is being rude in simple terms, and if I wasn't doing the right thing by managing my levels properly, I was sure to be thirsty to have the last word with a wise remark with whomever, which often got me in trouble with my parents. I didn't want to repeat that with my teacher. I programmed my mind to believe that there is a loophole in most situations, and if I could sense one, I was going to find it! As I reminisced about my 6th-grade teacher and her students on the first day of school, I thought, *"Ok, this is definitely not the "C" class."*

The saying goes, *"First impressions are the last impressions,"* and waiting for my instructor to arrive, the teacher's first impression was locked, and I was shocked by what my eyes noticed. My teacher, who arrived over an hour late to work, approached the classroom door to unlock it when I noticed six piercings in one ear, five in the other, a nose ring, her hair was purple and pink, and her sleeve tattoos were visible as well! I was shocked to see a teacher dressed in this fashion, but it was clear that she didn't want to be on school grounds like her students. Her body language spoke out loud in the silence, and silence does produce its own noise. Miss "Bora" rarely gave the students homework, and when she did, my mother and grandmother thought I would eventually develop a hernia because my book bag was exceedingly heavy. One day, I came into class, and my teacher stated for the students to take out their homework, and as she went around the classroom, she instructed the students one by one to enlighten the classroom of their answers received from the homework assignment. I thought to myself, *"Uh oh, I didn't do it!"* This side of the elementary school was a new addition to the school grounds, and landline phones were installed in the teacher's classroom.

If a student acted out, the teacher could call their parents in the classroom and embarrass the student among their peers. When it was my turn to provide my answer, I replied, *"I'm checking my blood sugar right now."* Ms. Bora brought me aside and asked, *"What did your teacher do last year?"* I informed her that I was just diagnosed with diabetes last month, so my teacher last year didn't do anything. Just because I was in the *"F"* class didn't mean I wasn't clever enough to pull a rabbit out of this hat. She then contacted the school nurse, and

I was instructed to exit the classroom and head toward the nurse's office. And it was at that moment I found the loophole.

When Ms. Bora would arrive hours late or have a *"no show,"* her students had to be divided into other classes, and I recall going into Mrs. G's class and having a spelling B with a few students from the *"F"* class and around thirty students from this *"C"* class, and I came in second place. It was gratifying knowing that I was still a smart kid, spelling words I had never studied, and this enabled me to feel empowered because knowledge is power!

Later that evening, Dad came to pick Desiree and me up from the after-school program *"Latchkey,"* and as I looked outside the window, the Chinese take-out adjacent to the school was set on fire by some street thugs. Once we were picked up and started our commute home with dad, we saw a white sheet over a lifeless corpse on *Archer Avenue* due to a shooting. This was not the first shooting to occur on this block while we were with him. The first time was a few years back, but as we were walking that street, we went to turn the corner, and dad pulled Desiree and me back as a gunshot was fired! He had to poke his head around the corner to make sure we would not be in a crossfire and to ensure we were cleared to continue towards the school.

The danger seemed to be increasing, and once we arrived home, my parents both agreed that we needed to relocate to a safer environment! Until this was set in motion, Desiree and I would have to continue getting picked up at a late hour from school, remaining in *Latchkey*. The teacher instructing this program was biased, and I grew angry at Mr. "Robins." I told him that Mr. L put his hands on me and I was going to report it to the principal! Since Mr. Robins and I disagreed aggressively, this was not going to get resolved since he was refusing to listen to me and was shielding his colleague. He eventually shouted, *"You're out of latchkey,"* and I replied with intensity, *"I don't care, and I'll do my homework at Kips Bay."* Kips Bay was another after-school program where the children could play video games, checkers, air hockey, board games and ping pong! This evening I told my mother that Mr. L punched me very hard on my arm in the gym. I wasn't into sports, so pardon me if I do not understand the rules, but there's no need for a gym teacher to strike a student! Robins was talking with my mother on the house phone, and she was getting loud with him until he stated that I yelled at the other teacher. Wait, what? How did this table just turn?

If somebody assaulted you, would you react in a positive or negative way? I felt flushed and had no idea what was going to happen, and the reason I felt like this was because towards the conclusion of this conversation, my mom said, *"Mmm hmmm… yeah… he did? Ok! Ok, Mr. Robins, thank you for calling! Bye!"* Like hypoglycemia, I felt faint and knew what was going to take place momentarily. Exiting her bedroom, she paced in my direction, and I grew clenched. Mom raised my right arm and spanked me for yelling at the gym teacher, and I didn't see that coming! When I tried running, she grabbed my ear and continued spanking me. I felt like a victim on this day, I was assaulted twice, and neither party apologized for their actions! I felt *imprisoned by torment* on this day and was a frantic child with a broken spirit and grew rancorous as time advanced. Being freed from dad's wrath now positioned mom to whoop my ass without remorse. She was supposed to be my soft place to fall on for difficult times.

In November of 1996, the family and I moved *Upstate,* but Michael was in college, so he remained in The *Bronx*! I was disillusioned about relocating because the brotherly advice that I may need down the line would no longer be available, and I had to relinquish my friendships, so I commenced feeling alone. I was a bold, bitter, foul mouth and anxious ill kid with low self-esteem and many insecurities, but I just wanted to be accepted. The more I believed I needed to demonstrate myself to be acknowledged, the more I felt unsatisfied. I had less than six months remaining of the sixth grade and continued to still find life challenging. Once I entered the new school, I commonly visited the nurse because my diabetes was by no means stable. I remember my neighbor Jerry saying, *"I want to be a diabetic,"* and I questioned, *"Why?"* he responded, *"Because every time I see you at the nurse's office, you always have soup, broth, or a diet Snapple beverage!"* Although I was not often taking care of myself for lack of caring, I did manage to somehow pass the sixth grade by the skin of my teeth with an overall average of 65.

Middle school wasn't any easier because my height, ailment, and attitude were all off from what was identified as *"normal."* As the shortest person on the school grounds, I was made fun of by the other students and my attitude while being ill was defiant. I just wanted to go through the school year in peace and pass without complications or cussing at people for their nonsense bullying. The students who did not experience life-altering challenges had an advantage over me and could never understand my trauma since my brain was focusing on survival, whereas their brain was free to grow and develop. Some students vocalized that they had earned my respect for being the smallest kid with one of the biggest hearts, always fighting with the will to survive, but the will to survive was one thing, and the will to manage this disease was another. The insecurities of being short suddenly didn't bother me, at least not at this moment, and I felt confident because of their edification.

I joined a juvenile diabetic support group at the middle school to get myself on track and felt comfortable as I realized that I was not the only kid dealing with this disease. As the year continued, my dad said, *"Let's get a dog for Steven."* We already had Zoe, and she's Desiree's dog, not mine. My family and I went to the pet shop in our local mall and began looking for who would be my best friend. My father noticed this one dog that looked like a complete mess but still asked, *"What about him?"* I looked around, and once I went back and forth a few times, the schnauzer my dad questioned locked eyes with me, and I knew I was about to have the best dog in that store! It worked out well because this puppy was a miniature schnauzer like Zoe, and he was the cheapest in price. My parents did not pay $200 for him; I did, and this was the Genesis of a new chapter that was ready to launch. I pretty much adopted him, was given the paperwork and this was now my baby boy, and his name is Max. I continued with my life but was still lackadaisical in managing my diabetes and yet passed another school year with an overall average of 65.

The next school year was great. However, meandering in the back of my mind was the concept of diabetes hindering my potential to excel. Since diabetes had control over me instead of me having control over it, my will to remain strong started to decrease. When taller students bullied me on school grounds, it always triggered my blood sugar to elevate. I felt hopeless and weak, couldn't fight back, and couldn't get even. I felt lost in an empty shell, and many things disturbed me. I felt as if I was a soda can that was shaken up, and the pressure within me just wanted to burst out! I didn't ask God to make me vertically challenged, so for people to ridicule me for something outside my reach was truly repulsive! I started to not care about my health due to the cycle of vitriolic attacks from others, so I began consuming anything I desired so that I would be vacant from everybody, resting in the nurse's office!

Aside from this, the year 1998 was pretty cool because, for the first time ever, I was going to experience a flight to *Florida*. The trip involved going to *"Space Camp"* for *Sesame Street,* and since Desiree was a normal character on the show, I was invited to be on this episode. I enjoyed my stay in *Florida*, and it was my *"get out of school"* card. My family and I had fun while traveling in unison, and I had the opportunity to view what it is that NASA does with astronauts and how they control the command center. I was also given a chance to have astronaut ice cream, and it was not cold but *"melted,"* almost like cotton candy. My blood sugar zip-lined over 500 since I was eating the non-sugar-free astronaut ice cream, and I should've known better, not that they had any that were dieting anyway. Mom made sure that my blood-sugar dropped while I rested. Since this diabetic situation transpired, I missed out on appearing in a few scenes of this episode but still got paid, so I wasn't going to bellyache over it, and once this whole segment of an event concluded, I was ready to go home!

Later that school year, there was a *Washington D.C.* trip that I was excited to attend, and I had my buddies Jerry, Sean, and Randy as my roommates. Jerry and Sean broke the seat hinge on the Coach Bus as one was leaning back to squash the other, and the other was kicking forward. During the moment it was funny, but as with anything in life, there is an equal reaction for every action. Someone got reprimanded harshly by their parents, and I was thrilled that it wasn't me. I was looking forward to experiencing the cruise, but the *"roller coaster effect"* was about to bestow me with its presence and fluster me in a massive way. I had a girlfriend at the time, and many people thought that Tanya and I were one of the cutest couples in school, but she had a spark in her eye for another student. The greatest panic received this year was from a kid, *"Rick,"* a tyrant who stood over six feet tall and was quite the issue. He despised me primarily because I didn't show him fear, and because of that, he would try to catch me in the hallways to assault me, and that's because I was an easy target. Well, Rick found me on the boat, and once he discovered my whereabouts, I wanted to just be with Tanya and enjoy the event, but Rick had another tactic in mind. My blood sugar started to spike, and I began feeling claustrophobic, like there was nowhere for me to go. I still couldn't find my girlfriend and thought that I was going to get hurt badly, but I would not panic until danger presented itself, and once this student proceeded to put his hands on me, he hung me over the boat and was ready to release me until he was spotted by a chaperone, stating he was only playing around with me. My insulin fell out of my pocket and went on a deep-sea diving exhibition. I wanted Dad here because I feared for my life, and approximately ten minutes later, I finally saw Tanya.

As she approached me, I felt slightly better until the news of her breaking up with me came into effect, and my eyes released a floodgate of tears. She apologized, and before she went about pursuing her new potential boyfriend, Desiree approached us and said, *"You two look so cute. Let me take a photo!"* Once the flash appeared, time froze, and my heart sank like an anchor! Desiree did not observe the breakup. I felt alone, and within me was another ticking time bomb. I felt as if I was following down some path of darkness with struggles and felt gravely ill from all that emerged, and I just wanted to go home since my glucose level elevated over 600! Diabetes was not easy for me to manage, even if I was eating the right nutrients.

Rick had to be picked up by a relative to return to *New York* since he was not permitted to return on the bus after that act of insubordination. I wanted my dog in my arms and this trip to be over because this eighth-grade experience turned out to be tremendously horrible for me! Once the school year was over, I had to attend summer school, which didn't bother me since this opportunity cost $10. I fortunately passed and was ready for senior high, and prior to autumn season beginning, Mom had summoned me inside our home and questioned, *"Steven wasn't that your sixth-grade teacher?"* I walked into her bedroom, looked at the television and confirmed my former sixth-grade teacher from *The Bronx* on the screen. She was terminated because of the usage of substances on school grounds, and when I think about the first time I met Ms. Bora, the pieces to the puzzle now formed in unity on why she was what she was demonstrating. She was clearly not hooked on Phonics but rather something quite addictive and deadly! I didn't see that coming!

CHAPTER 4

FRESHMAN/SOPHOMORE YEARS

I was trying to make a name for myself during freshmen year and often equated myself to others for self-evaluation. I was trying to do what was right since I knew I had difficulties, but I even wished on multiple occasions to run away! I knew I couldn't run away, and although death from diabetes would be a terrible *"escape"* from this world, it was not the answer to any problems I endured, and I'm pret0 sure that would've caused a lot of hearts to break and that's a one-way ticket to hell. Analyzing my role provided me with the determination to get ready for a fight, and with that fire burning, I was driven not to meet my demise at a young age! Fighting for my life daily was a full-time job, and school was secondary.

My brother decided to become a Marine because someone said he couldn't do it, and I understood that willpower of determination!

Michael also fought overseas. As I started to view how blue I was becoming, circumstances had to be adjusted, and I wanted to be appreciated and not feel isolated, so what was I going to do to become recognized? What abilities was I blessed with that I did not yet discover? Jerry, my neighbor and best friend, was always interested in playing video games with me and hanging out, which provided a smile on my face. One day he and I were playing with a frisbee, and it landed on the roof of his home, and since I'm petite, I stated that I would retrieve it. Jerry's mother pulled into their driveway moments after being on the roof and was spotted by her. After my feet were planted on the ground, his mom told me that she has to tell my parents about this, and Jerry retorted to his mother that she would be doing no such thing because if she did, I would've been in some serious hot water. Jerry prevented a possible punishment, and I was grateful for his loyalty to our friendship but let me just say that if I had spoken to my mother the way Jerry did to his mom, I might not be alive, ha-ha.

When in doubt, man's best friend will always prevail, and he definitely provided me with the love required to fulfill this current void. After rough days of school, I couldn't wait to be homebound to see him, and no matter what type of day I would encounter, Max was the most loving dog and was where I found my relief. The most fun I had at my parent's residence was either playing my video games, viewing game shows, watching wrestling, or playing around with Max. He even knew what *"Give me a hug"* meant, always placing his head on my chest when I requested a hug, and this always brought a smile to my face considering Max hugged me more than anybody. When diabetes made me ill, Max never left my side, and I had to focus on my schoolwork this year, but history would repeat itself. I was not putting my health before all else, and diabetes had full control over me, altering my attitude. It also didn't help that I had shingles and that alone was painful.

I would try to win people's acceptance to be noticed instead of managing my diabetes. I was known as the short diabetic who was always in the nurses' office but was sick and tired of being sick and tired and told myself that I couldn't keep repeating this mundane lifestyle. My overall average was below 65 because I was not managing my diabetes again, and I didn't want to get left behind because graduating without my twin would haunt me forever! I failed this year miserably, and the ultimatum was to repeat the 9th grade in summer school, which was $200 or be placed in a Special Ed program for the sophomore year. I decided to enjoy my Summer and return to sophomore year in what was called the *"Oasis Program."*

My guidance counselor introduced me to the staff and the students of the Oasis Program. As I saw the class in session, I stated, *"I don't belong here!"* but every student in this program had a reason for why they were positioned here, so who was I to judge them for what could be holding them back? For me, it was my diabetes! This was a Special Ed class, so I had to expect people and things to be different from mainstream courses. Jermaine was the first student who made me feel content and even invited me to his dad's house to create music since he had the equipment. I didn't know what to think except that this could be fun, and Jermaine loved the rap industry, and I grew to like it as well. We found our common interest, plus the kickoff to a new friendship was established! Oasis was held in two classrooms in the corner of the high school, segregated from the mainstream classes, and what a thrill to know that homework was not given, but if it was, it was once a month, if that. I enjoyed both educators, but my favorite teacher of the two was Mr. Klopper! Talk about a laudable man, and in my opinion, no teacher on this campus fit the mold better of what a teacher should represent than Mr. Klopper! The best part about going to school was learning from his teachings. He was my role model, and I knew that on this day, fate was sealed and failing with my grades was no longer probable because this teacher was not going to allow me to fail! In essence, failure was not an option!

My sophomore year was different for many reasons. I was given the name *"The Pebble"* as a joke because I looked like *"The Rock"* according to a few, and eventually, the name *"LILROCK"* would come into effect since I could raise both my eyebrows like him and was even on the wrestling team. When an entire gym class chants *"Little Rock, Little Rock,"* you know something went right, and the name remained from that day forward! My will to succeed was advancing, and Mr. Klopper would provide me with many words of wisdom to further assist me with complications outside of school curriculums. I was driven to be successful, and Mr. Klopper offered me a lot of hope. I dated two women in this program for a brief while and realized that just because I was ill and short didn't mean I was not desired or attractive because I have character. One of these girls stood 5'11 and made me look extremely little, but it caught the eyes of many people. The other was different and just didn't take crap from anybody, and although things were going well in this program, nothing was ever perfect, and I still had to deal with my troubles. I recall one day feeling faint and wanting to come home to rest. My dad was working overnights, and on this day, I was not required to stay in school since I was not well. The nurse contacted my house and explained the situation to my dad, stating that I should be home resting due to my condition. My dad was willing to call a cab to pick me up, but Mrs. Bumbolow explained that this was not possible because he had to sign me out, and the signature had to be from a parent or guardian.

The Summer prior, I showed dad how close of proximity the high school was to our home, and since he now knew the trail of direction towards the school, he commenced his walk to get me, and once he signed me out, my dad stated in the nurse's office, *"Let's get walking"*, as if it was that simple for me. Mrs. B replied, staggered, *"Mister Casado, exercise will only elevate his sugar level."* As my dad grabbed my book bag, I looked at Mrs. B and moved my lips, without vocals saying that I will be fine. My dad has had an alcohol problem most of his life, so he never obtained a license. He knew if he did, he would've been standing before God long ago because of drunk driving. Smart man! Dad passed my diet beverage over to me, and we exited the school and started our commute home, and once we arrived, I took more insulin, ingested some soup, and went to sleep!

Mid-school year, I started dating a girl whose name won't be mentioned, and I recall Jerry inviting me to Wednesday night bible study for the teenagers and thought that this would be different and perhaps even fun. Jerry obtained his license and questioned if I wanted to tag along. I wanted to join because I had the ability to leave my house, my best friend wanted me to ride with him in his first purchased vehicle, and I would be attending bible study with my girlfriend, who Jerry informed me would be there. The cluster of high school kids that attended this bible study was willing to learn about the gospel every week. If they enjoyed something like this, the question was *"Why?"* so I wanted to attend more sessions to understand what they understood!

The gospel message was presented clearly on a weekly basis, and I received much wisdom from the teachings involved with this class during the times I was present and was willing to listen since these subjects were never discussed at home. My father believed that I was out drinking and doing drugs on these Wednesday evenings, and although I could've been, those thoughts never meandered in my mind! A corrupt conscience will always see a negative situation in a positive concept because that's the baggage they carry! Jerry and I would go to the local school once a month on Friday night to participate in a pizza/basketball event with church leaders and other high school students. It was pleasant to fellowship, play and listen to more of the good news from Joe, a godly man who organized this recreational time to be very eventful and intriguing. I believe that Joe planted the first seed of courage in me, but that seed needed watering and sunlight! I perceived my determination in life with the good news Joe provided every chance he could, with the Holy Spirit guiding him, and I told myself that I would be an improved individual. However, this was hormone season, and my body said otherwise!

Once I turned sixteen, this would be the age where I experienced the first of many concepts, and a few were destructive as I was rebellious for many reasons. Before these notions would occur, my mother was kind enough to drive Desiree and me with our grandmother to *Hershey Park* for our birthday. As a diabetic, the setting concerned me, but once we arrived, it was moderately easy to resist the temptation of extra sweets, knowing my life would be in jeopardy! Desiree and I were explorative at the park and relished this birthday gift in unity, and it concluded with the outdoor laser show, which was phenomenal. When we departed from the park and headed back home the following day, I created a minor list of tasks to complete; to feel appreciated, fulfilled, and proficient at my accomplishments. Now that I'm sixteen, I'm ready to find hobbies, determined to prove myself and ready for whatever adventure lies ahead! I constructed an ego in the process of trying to do good, but that drove me to be disrespectful in some areas because everything was about me and what I could do! Down the street from my residence were two young kids, George and Kristie, who love me as an older brother. I enjoyed looking out for them, but their mother and I hated each other during this time because I would always speed down the road, put my gear in neutral and rev the engine to let George know that I was homebound.

This was also his idea, and I always received a text message from either George or Kristie every night when I passed their home. George was another best friend, and we hung out every weekend, and there were times when I'd stay over and just have a blast chilling with him! My connection with them both was between us, and I cared little for their neighbors' opinions. I literally saw nothing wrong with what I was doing. The thing is, you can't modify what you don't acknowledge, and nobody told me anything except their mother, who bought a yellow sign and wrote, *"Slow Down,"* and when she held it on this particular day, I flipped her off!

Moonlight bowling became my weekend activity and was for many years. One night I saw this girl Kim, and we stood about the same height, which was cute, and although I was being flirtatious, I didn't act on anything because I already had a girlfriend. A month later, Jerry saw Kim sitting on my lap inside the bowling alley, and because he liked my girlfriend, Jerry called her and informed her of what was transpiring. I understood why he did what he did, but as one of my best friends and neighbor, that was a low blow. I wasn't cheating on my girlfriend, nor did I think conversing like this at the bowling alley was a big deal because there were six of us, four seats to a table, and Kim wanted to sit on my lap. My number one fear is rejection, and my number one need is acceptance! What a conundrum!

Jerry wanted what I had, and he was successful! She eventually broke up with me and started dating him. This suppressed fuel of rage for a while, and my friendship with Jerry was temporarily lacerated because of a female. Approximately two weeks later, during 4th period, I was sitting in the school cafeteria when this guy Duane walked towards the lunch table where I sat and stated that there was a girl who was interested in dating me. After getting to know her, I dated *"Sandra"* for a short while and was actually desired! This was the sensation I sought to be fulfilled, and once I experienced it, I didn't want to lose it. I've often mentioned that I felt *"I needed to be needed";* otherwise, what was the point of my purpose? A lot of females were calling my house to speak with me, and on this day, my dad bellowed at the last caller and said, *"I told you he's not here,"* and hung up on Sandra, the last caller! I was walking home, and I heard this personally when I arrived. My dad told me that someone called five times looking for me, but it turns out that all 5 callers were different females as I looked at the caller ID! My dad said he thought it was the same person calling repeatedly and apologized for his actions. Well, because of this, I was dumped the following day! Tick-Tock!

As the school year progressed, my grades were getting better, but I still felt like an outcast. I would feel repulsed from drinking anything sugar-free, so I said, *"I'm damned if I do and damned if I don't,"* and remained drinking beverages that contained regular sugar instead of training myself to do without it. I managed my diabetes irresponsibly, and for every action, there is an equal reaction. I was about eighty pounds soaking wet, so to see myself drinking a diet beverage would make me appear odd, and I wasn't trying to have this image. I was insecure about many things, and I didn't want to give the impression that I was abnormal, so I became a product of my environment; that way, I didn't feel excluded from anything. My thoughts were, *"As long as my blood-sugars are stable, everything will be fine,"* but actions speak louder than words, and if I'm drinking non-diet beverages to appear *"normal"* to others, I was only deceiving myself and indirectly, self-inflicting, negative vibes, thoughts, and physical harm to my body due to glucose levels rising for whatever I was consuming.

In due time I started dating Kim and was no longer dreading my past. The State Trooper on school grounds was cool, and I had two encounters with him; one was funny during a serious matter, and the other worked in my favor. I had an extremely high blood-sugar one day for foolishly drinking two 20-ounce bottles of Snapple and was strolling through the hall with my head hung and right arm extended on the wall to hold me up. A student questioned if I was ok, considering I looked deathly ill! Since I was feeling like death, my mind wasn't clear when I spoke, and I uttered, *"I'm high. I need to go shoot my needle in my arm!"* The student appeared disturbed, expressed to the Trooper the scenario and minutes later, he saw me walking through the hall. The Trooper said that I did not look well and voiced, *"You look high,"* and I retorted, *"You know about diabetes?"* We chuckled about it because he saw how the story got misconstrued, and I was about to throw up because of my illness. I went to the nurses' office, and Mrs. Bumbolow checked my sugar level.

The glucometer said *"High,"* indicating that my sugar was over 600. I was escorted out on a stretcher, and when my blood was taken at the hospital, my glucose was 1392. The nurse at the hospital stated, *"The only reason you're still alive is because of your youth, and if you keep doing this, you'll die by twenty-four!"* I took those words as my sword and shield and told myself that I would survive all scenarios because I'm young! Once a glucose number reaches the level of 800, this now becomes the *"Diabetic Coma"* zone. When I returned home, I weighed myself and lost 10 pounds from that morning because of this occurrence at school. My cells were feeding off the little body fat I had, and it was at a rapid pace, allowing me to understand why I felt like my life was draining from my body.

Jerry's girlfriend wrote me a virtual message on *AOL Instant Messenger,* and I printed the conversation on the school premises to show him what was being expressed to me from her screenname. When I disclosed this to him, Jerry did not believe the proof provided for his eyes to see and then stated that there was a conversation that he, too, had printed out, and when I observed it, I stated that I did not do this! He didn't believe me, so a sigh released from within me as I proceeded to walk away displeased. The State Trooper got involved as he observed the entirety of this altercation as both Jerry, and I were in the cafeteria. The Trooper stated that he would contact *AOL* to see if this and the other conversation were legit and if either were bogus, the individual who made up their conversation will lose any scholarship they were trying to receive. Jerry suddenly obtained a pensive look, and we parted ways.

Jerry was exposed to the truth days later and apologized, discovering that what I printed was not fraudulent. However, he did reveal to me that the *"conversation"* he gave to the Trooper was indeed bogus, as I was already aware of, and our friendship was restored. I was just happy to not have to punch him in his kneecap again because years prior, Jerry asked if I was going to punch him in his knee for beating me in a wrestling video game, so I briefly thought about it, clenched my fist, and struck a blow to his kneecap and it hurt him more than he thought it would, and Jerry expressed that he'll never joke like that with me again. Hahaha, I don't enjoy being bullied.

As stated previously, once I became 16 years of age, many *"firsts"* were going to occur, and my first objective was obtaining a license! I also wanted to work so I could rely on myself and purchase what I desired since an allowance wasn't received at home. However, my dad occasionally provided me with a few bucks here and there, and I appreciated Dad's contribution because he told me that he could go buy alcohol but would rather give me the money, which I thought was awesome. I also thought that I would feel loved and appreciated if I had a long-term relationship! The day I went for my road test, I passed and felt very accomplished, and my first car was a 1996 Red Dodge Neon, and my buddy Duane tagged along to *Connecticut* with me to pick up the vehicle. I began to experience the privilege of being a driver, and once I received this vehicle that my mother purchased for me, I wanted to just drive and be free!

My friend Sean who was on the *D.C.* trip, is the type of guy who loves working on cars, and wanted to detail my vehicle, so I granted him the opportunity. He used spray cans to paint the air vents, panels, and radio board black and red, and on the front window, I had decals put on which said *"LILROCK"* in white lettering. Sean went about spraying the hub caps, gas cap, and both side mirrors white. In addition, he purchased red chrome windshield wipers, so my car looked immaculate. I was standing out and felt like a champion!

My first occupation was working at the local mall at a movie theater where I sold tickets at the box office, and as a diabetic, I was not trying to labor myself in the concession stand for obvious reasons, but that didn't stop me from having cherry slushies which is a big no-no to people with diabetes. My occupation allowed me to interact with people of different races, ages, and religions which was now the kickoff of me starting to build a background in customer service! The collaboration with many people permitted me to learn how to address individuals of all types. I wanted to excel in all I was accomplishing, so to be told *"Good job"* or *"Well done"* at least half the time I worked permitted me to feel very content.

Growing up, I often heard *"No"* or *"You can't do that,"* which are not words of encouragement, so I took any compliment thrown in my direction with open arms. I recall a young female flirting with me while I was at the box office, and she was exceptionally attractive and even asked if I would date her! As much as I wanted to say yes, I was loyal to my faithfulness and expressed to her that I was already in a relationship. I knew she only wanted to date me so she could come to the movies for free. When I went to work, my ego was often boosted, just like my blood sugar, and neither was beneficial. I was great at my occupation but was still failing at the job of taking care of my diabetes!

My relationship with Kim lasted a year and a half, and during this time, it was blissful to find someone who enjoyed my company. We often went to the bowling alley or mall or simply drove around just because I was blessed with a vehicle to do so, and Kim wanted to introduce me to her friend Danielle. I drove to Danielle's residence and met her and her boyfriend. These two individuals showed a great deal of respect for someone they never encountered prior to this day! I exchanged numbers with *"Ceccil,"* then Kim and I vacated the premises, and many of my *"firsts"* commenced in this relationship! I despised the idea of people smoking, nor did I want to comprehend the concept of inhaling smoke and chemicals into my lungs to be *"at ease."*

My girlfriend happened to smoke, and it irritated me until I morphed into a product of my environment. I was standing in her living room when she sparked a lighter to smoke a cigarette, and in a passive-aggressive manner, I told her that if she smoked the cigarette, I would take one and do the same. She continued, so I grabbed one, and she said, *"Steve, stop it!"* Once I took my first drag, not only did she take it, but she followed up with a light smack across my face. I responded collectively for her to give it back; otherwise, I might get a little upset. I was already a hot mess with anger, so that would not have been cool! I was now a smoker at 16 years of age and was purchasing them from a store that I knew would not ask me for identification because of how I presented myself.

There was an afternoon when I went to Kim's house and was playing the video game *"Sonic 2,"* and she asked me if I wanted to smoke pot and expressed to me that since I now smoke cigarettes, I would enjoy this activity. I was reluctant until wrestling was broadcasted on television, and now, I didn't have a care in the world. We smoked, and I became a baked potato, and at some point, Kim asked me, *"Want a shotty?"* I answered, *"Sure, sure... what's a shotty?"* She started laughing, as did I, for I had no idea what was happening or what was about to occur. I now understood why it was called *"a shotty"* because I was absolutely freaking shot! A shotty is when you connect your pointer finger with your thumb, then lock your middle, ring and pinky with the other individual. Kim placed the blunt in her mouth and between her pointer finger and thumb and exhaled while my mouth was cuffed around my pointer finger and thumb while inhaling the smoke. Yep, I was as high as a giraffe's butt and that's about 6 feet high up. I felt really elevated.

I enjoyed her company, and after this smoke fest took place, another first was about to set itself in place. As my sinful heart wanted to have an intimate encounter, the feeling was mutual, and that is exactly what happened. This was a bad call on my behalf because there was a cause and effect here. Since I'd never performed either of these activities prior to this evening, I didn't know I would be so physically drained that I would pass out watching wrestling. The idea was to go home after wrestling concluded, as this was a common routine, but I never made it home that evening. The next morning, my mother called my cellphone, but I was out like a light and did not respond.

She knew where I was because my car was not in our driveway, so she drove by Kim's house and spotted my vehicle parked outside her household. Mom proceeded to call Kim's mother, who answered her landline phone, and I heard, *"Yes, he's here! I had no idea."* My mom was not trying to hear what happened or what excuse I would give her, and that was fine until she told me to give her the car keys.

A few days passed, and Kim introduced me to her cousins. I knew one of the two and felt peer pressure because of the question that would be asked, and my conscience knew that I needed to make an optimal decision. I was asked if I drank alcohol, and I replied that I did not. My judgment was compromised by allowing myself to believe that doing anything my girlfriend wanted would make her *"happier,"* but that was far from the veracity. Going against my own judgment, I began drinking just for this social gathering but would not allow myself to make this into a habitual manner. I was unaware that consuming alcohol would trigger my blood sugar to spike, so again, I was indirectly self-inflicting harm to my body. Tick-Tock!

While in Oasis, I was still involved with Kim and towards the end of my year-and-a-half relationship, I found out that she cheated on me with another person with the same name as me, and he was supposed to be one of my comrades. She wrote it in her diary, and I wasn't trying to be inquisitive, but she left the book wide open, and I saw my name from afar and grew curious about what was being expressed about me. Once the secret was revealed, I was emotionally wounded because of how devoted I was to her. I provided all I could for Kim, but my best was not good enough. The relationship ended on a sour note, but I already had someone waiting to date me, so I was dreading nothing!

As the year continued, I continued to excel in many areas, and the Oasis program was the reason for this being a possibility. The two teachers conducting these classes had to have much patience with their students, and they executed this task very well. The end of the sophomore year concluded with me passing with flying colors, and I knew that this was my opportunity to do what I thought was not possible, and that was passing the school year with ease. Now that I knew I could accomplish this task, nobody nor anything was going to convince me otherwise! A few times during the Summer, Jermaine and I would hang out, write music and record it simply because we said we could and encouraged each other to be better, just the same way we successfully passed the school year by helping each other!

CHAPTER 5

MANY TRANSITIONS

I was determined to walk into the junior year with a different attitude, and when Oasis took note that I was healthy enough to partake in a mainstream course, I was positioned in a math class and had to keep myself in check because the last time Mrs. O was my teacher, I was very rude to her and was banished from her class permanently during freshman year! My elevated glucose levels often played a significant role in why I was vitriolic or blue. I recall the astonished expression on the teacher's face when I was always willing to answer her math questions with the breakdown on why that is the answer, while trying not to be a goody-two-shoes.

For the first time since kindergarten, I was in the same classroom as Desiree and immediately questioned silently, *"Is this the "A" class?"* and wanted to show in general that the new me was different, had goals and wanted to prove the change! The first week of school was great, and I was doing well on who I was becoming instead of making excuses because excuses are just well-thought-out lies! As I was attentive to myself, I felt I was tasked to lead by example to those in my circle.

The second week of school left an unpleasant stain of grief for thousands, as a current event would leave a permanent scar for many to endure. I was in Mr. Klopper's classroom when a student in the hallway shouted, *"A plane just went into the Trade Center!"* Once I heard that *Manhattan* would be evacuating, I could only think about my family who worked in the city or who lived in *Staten Island*, like my Aunt Mady and Uncle Chris. My aunt happened to be on the ferry and saw the attack with her own eyes. *Manhattan* is known as *"The city that never sleeps."* It was a frightening image from a helicopter view to see not a single body in *Time Square* because of the evacuation.

Michael was in *Afghanistan*, and when this attack occurred, I thought about his well-being in hopes that he was protected and doing well with his fellow troops. I recall speaking with him on the phone, and although Mom demanded I not tell him the problems that were occurring at home, I had my reasons for telling him everything because I could never voice my opinion without repercussions. I don't recall the details of what Mom and I were confrontational about, except that it had to do with my car in her name, and I was getting tired of the control and her trying to strip me of the gift she purchased for me. It wasn't like I was getting speeding tickets or anything, I made a mistake.

Mom was standing at twelve o'clock to me in the kitchen while Dad was at four o'clock, about five feet away, and then she approached my face while yelling at me and ripped the gold chain she bought me for my birthday off my neck. I shouted, *"You broke my chain!"* and clenched my teeth and fist, and she responded, *"It's not yours. I bought it!"* I looked towards my right, and Dad dared me to strike her; if I did, he said he would knock me out! When a person or people are not guided by the Holy Spirit, they are consumed with the nonsense of the world and its attitude and my parents needed the guidance from a Higher Being, as did I.

Now, I was never going to assault my mother but was now contemplating attacking Dad just for threatening me. In a quick glance, I thought about all the wrestling submission moves I could perform but also knew that I wasn't trying to look like a menace if I performed what I envisioned in my brain because if I did, I would've been arrested! The apple doesn't fall far from the tree and my attitude is now building worse than Dad's in my opinion, I just know how to contain it. Therapy sessions could have been useful right about now, but I needed brotherly advice at this point. How could I not tell Michael about this chaos that took place in our home? So, when I told him that mom said not to say anything, he replied, *"Nah bro bs, you tell me anything you want! I'm defending your freedom; the first amendment is freedom of speech, so speak your mind!"*

Mom was not wrong for saying what she voiced, but it also wasn't right, and although freedom isn't free, I have one blood brother, and nobody will dictate what I verbalize to him! I felt like a war was happening everywhere, and Michael was concerned for me as I was for him because of the terrorist attack that just took place! Many lives were affected, and this would make a devastating mourning for the time to come.

The next relationship I invested my time in would last sixteen months and was a waste of time, as history would repeat itself for dating another unfaithful person! This time the dishonesty was with a female, but deceitfulness is deceitfulness, no matter how you slice it! During this period, *"DeeDee"* and I were working at *A.C. Moore* together, and it was challenging to labor myself on work grounds yet still manage the frames department. I questioned a coworker if he wanted to go on break with me, and he agreed that he was overdue for one anyway, so I bought some scratch-offs and kept going back and forth, winning and losing. I told the clerk at the register, *"I'm going to get another dollar from my car to buy that ticket, my friend!"* I went to my vehicle, grabbed four quarters, and walked back inside the gas station.

My coworker purchased the scratch-off I was going to buy and won $1,000 for life! I was struck with paralysis and engulfed in turmoil because that was the ticket I was going to purchase, and it was swept right underneath my feet, and I felt raided! I had a sourpuss expression on my face and felt ransacked out of a relationship and now finances. I returned to work irritated because homeboy quit right there, and I had to channel my aggression into a positive but was unaware of how to do this task! Seriously, I was fuming. Tick-Tock!

Focusing on my education, my class schedule for junior year was great because I had gym during 6th period, lunch in 7^{th,} and study hall in 8th. After gym class on this one particular day, I was walking with a group of students from the outdoor track towards the school, where a teenager was laying on the concrete with students surrounding him with no awareness of how to respond. I approached him swiftly and questioned what was wrong, and *"I'm hypoglycemic, and my blood sugar is very low"* rolled off his tongue, so I told him I would return quickly.

Lunch was $1.75, and I took the only two dollars in my pocket and ran inside the cafeteria to grab this student a soda. I ran to the nurse's office and said, *"Mrs. B, follow me outside towards the cafeteria."* I grabbed the wheelchair and hasted my way to him! Once Mrs. Bumbolow got everything situated, she told me that Lee would be okay and contacted his aunt and uncle, who told Mrs. B they would meet him at the hospital. I told the nurse that I didn't have any more classes for the remainder of the day, so I'll accompany him until his guardians arrived at the hospital. I bolted off the school campus to get in my car and trail behind the ambulance and grew excited about many reasons, such as leaving school early, speeding through red lights with the rescue team in front of me, and I was gaining a new friendship in the process. Lee's uncle expressed gratitude towards me, and I was invited to come over to his home to have dinner and watch wrestling on his 60-inch television. Lee and I often hung out after this occurrence took place and remained good friends!

Down the timeline, *Thanksgiving Eve* was the day when a substantial change would arise in my life, and as I recall dad coming home drunk, I became ticked off as a result of his actions. What actions? My room was torn upside down, my speakers from my sound system were hanging by their connected cords just dangling, my television wasn't where it was originally, and I had no desire to fix it since I wanted him to view what he accomplished while being intoxicated!

The next morning, my sister and I went to *Manhattan* with Mom since Desiree was in the *"Macy's Thanksgiving Day Parade"* with the cast of *Sesame Street*. As my mother and I were waiting inside *Penn Station* for Desiree, I received a phone call from Dad at 8:23 a.m., picked up my phone, and he questioned in a calm manner where I was and what happened to my room. I expressed to him that I was sitting down inside *Penn Station,* and he was what had happened to my room. He retorted, *"I did that? I don't remember it! I'm sorry, Steve! I promise from this day forth, I will never drink another drop of alcohol again!"* This was the second promise my father made to me, and by the grace of God, he kept his word! Amen!

Dad told me that he devoted and surrendered his life to Jesus, and I didn't know what that meant, but if God could change such a man, that means that God is still in the business of miracles! I was also not certain how my life would change, but I braced myself to see what would happen next, considering my entire life, I was raised catholic and followed a religion that says it's okay to do this and that, yet the Bible is very clear on its do's and do nots, so I was curious on how Dad would demonstrate this new image he was trying to represent. Dad wanted to search for a church to attend and after scouting for some time, Mom and Dad eventually found *The First Baptist Church of Peekskill* and became different beings, were striving to be better than what they were previously, and I was impressed because they both literally illuminated with a Light that I did not comprehend, and they looked alive and healthy too. 2 Corinthians 5:17 says, "Therefore if anyone is in Christ, he is a new creature; the old things have passed away; behold, new things have come."

When Desiree and I were twelve, our parents took us out to eat at a Pub, and my dad noticed two priests from the catholic church that we used to attend, in uniform, drinking alcohol and smoking cigarettes! It meandered in my dad's mind that this was not the leadership he wanted his kids to see because he was already doing these things, which is why he obscured our sight to witness them red-handed. He later vocalized what he observed, which is why I was now aware of this information. People who are viewed as a leader of any kind have a responsibility, and the truth is that "you can't change the people around you" in the sense of how they conduct themselves, but "you can change the people around you" and walk with an uplifting, optimistic attitude! Nonetheless, with my dad on his new venture, the thoughts meandering through my mind were that he was going to be a sober man but perhaps more aggressive about the do's and don'ts of life since he is now a believer! I didn't know how a believer was supposed to act as well, but my dad would allow his Father in heaven to have control over his life, and although I did not know what this meant, I noticed a different man in dad and said to myself that this would probably only be temporary.

The school year would be coming to an end, and because of *Oasis*, I passed with ease, and it was seriously the steppingstone for all that I would learn and achieve since this program had very well-trained teachers who performed at their finest! Mr. Klopper introduced the movie *"Les Miserables"* to the class, and this reformed my vision in a few aspects because of how well this film was produced, and the message within it was perfect! We concluded the motion picture in two days, and by that weekend, I owned the movie on DVD and expressed to Dad that he needed to watch this film. I gave a lot of acknowledgment to Mr. Klopper for who I was becoming since he was my teacher and showed a lot of great characteristics that I wanted to acquire, and the one that caught my attention the most was the minutiae of information he would provide to the students.

At this point in my education, I only needed to attend *Oasis* a few classes out of the school day. My favorite classes this year were oceanography and meteorology. I remember a couple of students stating that they did not want to partake in the dissection of the frog in biology class, and I never took biology because I failed earth science in 9th grade and had to repeat it in 10th grade. I asked Mr. Klopper if I could observe what they were doing, and he responded, *"Hey Steven if you'd like to involve yourself in this class, I'll give you the biology credit."* I seized the opportunity because I knew I could use the credit. Jermaine was excited to see me participate in this class, and my attitude this year was optimistic since I was focusing on not being weak but rather productive and useful. I would walk around the school with a laminated pass provided by the school nurse at the beginning of the third quarter and had the greatest perk, leaving any classroom, when necessary, without consent from a teacher to go manage my diabetes at the nurse's office. The hall monitors started referring to me as *"The Mayor of the School"* because I used it for its purpose while also using it to my advantage. The year did have its pros and cons, but I managed to pass my senior year with flying colors. The greatest moment I witnessed at the school year's conclusion was seeing my brother Michael in his Marine attire and in the presence of my family! Michael accomplished his four years, and I was not only very proud of his service but was also grateful to see him at graduation alive and well!

After graduating, my goal was to obtain a job that allowed me to interact with many people simultaneously. Jon, a friend of three years, was working at *RadioShack*, and as I was in the mall scouting for employment, he noticed me by the entrance of the store and stated that I should apply for the holiday season since they were looking for assistance. I strolled in and spoke with the hiring manager, and he recruited me on the spot since they were understaffed, and with the holiday season in motion, it was vital for them to acquire more employees. I went through my training, was certified, and am now equipped for the sales floor! For the first time in my life, I worked on *Black Friday*, which I had never heard of prior to this year, and since I was working with electronics, people wanted their hands on the hottest items. While working for this company, I was introduced to a young man named Silva, who is quite the character because of his silly personality. We discovered that we lived down the road from one another and eventually became best of friends! I always treasured the idea that some saw me as a brother, and most people knew me to be a reliable source. While working during the holiday season, I wanted to demonstrate to management that I was willing to work extra hours to maximize my working experience under pressure because of the holiday rush.

After two months with this company, I became a key holder; by the third month, I was the new Assistant Manager! Some details of my new tier required me to set up floor planograms and count and replenish inventory while training new employees and working on the sales floor off commission. The responsibilities opened my mind, and that leadership inside of me indicated that I was only going to be as good as I allowed myself to become and was looking to be that next coal squeezed into a diamond! I went to the haircutting shop in the mall and noticed my friend Andrew from middle school working there, and after that first cut, I knew who I would return to in order to keep my flawless fresh-looking appearance. I was so puffed up about this promotion that I decided to seek additional employment to build my resume and wanted to be the man who never requested money from others! Kim's cousin informed me that *Dunkin Donuts* was looking for morning assistance from six to noon and put in a good word for me. I obtained a second job and was zealous to be the man! I wanted to prove that I could do anything by saying *"I can"* and *"I will"* and let my performance speak for itself! *Many transitions were in motion!*

CHAPTER 6

WHAT I WANTED

One Friday evening, I recall being scheduled to work at RadioShack until 9:30 p.m. when a group of about a dozen teens strode into the store; and in that crowd, two of them seemed interested in a friendship because of how well I represented myself in confidence. The one who stood out the most was Adam, and after talking for a brief while, he questioned, *"Maybe we can hang out sometime? What's your name?"* I replied, *"Steve but my close friends call me LILROCK."* Adam had this charisma that intrigued me to see what he was about, and the feeling was mutual. The other young male named *"E"* who was with Adam asked me if I rapped and I told him that it wasn't my thing, but I have in the past! Growing up, I wasn't big on music, but what drew me towards rap music was the instrumentals, not the lyrics. It reminded me of Jermaine since he and I often listened to instrumentals. Hanging out with Adam and *"E"* permitted me to listen to music with no words again, and freestyling became a hobby! If you want to talk about talent, Adam is a golden key lyricist, and I was astonished to hear how he freestyled!

I was getting the recognition that I sought and enjoyed it exponentially because, in many people's views, I was a leader. I was their safe point and took the role of being an older brother. George, Kristie, and two others were going up to *Poughkeepsie* for an event at club *Intrigue,* which was only for teenagers on this night, and they needed a lift. I was at the end of my teen years and asked to participate since this will never be able to occur again! I agreed to drive George, Kristie, and two others about an hour North, and I had a blast with them, but of course, there's always someone willing to cause mischief of some kind, and Kristie fell victim at the club. She's an attractive blonde, and as I saw her dancing exuberantly with others, it irked me because Kristie had a lot of hyenas surrounding her. I just wanted to vibe well with my "brother" George and see a "sister" smile, and I had a hunch she was going to lose her grin.

My demeanor changed as I saw the thirst in these guys for her, their body language spoke volumes, and I just wanted to push an eject button on all of them. Kristie dressed to impress, and unfortunately one of these goons slipped their hand by her front waistline and unclipped her Nextel. This was a very common act with these phones, and it was unfortunate for those who became a target. When Kristie realized that her phone was stolen, we all attempted to get her phone back or retrieve another as a replacement. The only time two negatives equal a positive is when you multiply two negatives, and although the intent was there, we weren't successful!

I had a responsibility to these kids, and as long as they were under my guidance, I had to protect them like they were younger brothers or sisters. By the conclusion of this evening, Kristie didn't recover her phone or gain another in its place, George was drinking a bottle of something that he had brought with him, and one of the other guys had weed, and I was the responsible chauffeur who made sure all of them were dropped off safely because I'm a boss, and I'm just that guy!

As we began vacating the club, many of the other people who lived close to us were asking me for a ride since there were no more trains running during this late hour. I literally had no space, and one guy even suggested that I let him ride in my trunk, but I retorted, *"You're not my responsibility, bro. They are, and my sound system is there, and you won't fit!"* I felt terrible, but there was only so much I could provide. On our way home, I had put on my L.E.D lights so the car would look cool at night, but not knowing this was illegal; I was now getting pulled over by a State Trooper. The elderly officer asked to see my papers, noticed all parties in the car, and asked me to step out. Standing in front of his vehicle and on camera, he asked me a series of questions.

I answered them without hesitation, and then he questioned, *"You have anything illegal in your vehicle?"* I stated that I did not and was driving my neighbors and their friend's home from a club that was for teens this evening. The officer allowed me to leave, and when I returned to the car, George had his open bottle by his feet, and the others were waiting to roll up and smoke while Kristie was upset about her phone being stolen. I dropped everyone off safely and was somewhat grateful that this was not going to occur again since my teenage years were coming to an end!

Throughout this period, I didn't want to invest my time into doing foolish things, so I decided to attend college for computer graphics while simultaneously working these two occupations. The college was down the street from where Lee resided, so I would park my car in his uncles' driveway and walk towards the Community College. Upon my return, I'd have dinner with Lee's family, and afterward, he and I often played a wrestling game on the PS2. It was always competitive playing with Lee on the PlayStation, and I enjoyed it more because I knew how the game was created, considering I was in the midst of taking computer graphics. We eventually started playing *Yu-Gi-Oh*, and I valued playing this card game because it requires skill and strategy, and it could be quite a conundrum at times, so you have to plan ahead to be victorious, just like you would in chess. Anybody who knows me is fully aware that I love solving puzzles, especially in retail management, and when things went wrong, I needed to figure out why and resolve the problem! Lee was searching for employment, and I explained to him that he could work at a different *RadioShack* store since I knew the hiring manager.

He grabbed this opportunity and was hired, and then Michael asked me if I could get him into *RadioShack* as well. Unfortunately, because I was the Assistant Manager in my store, Michael could not be hired there, but I was able to plug him into a different location. Around this time, I was obsessed with lightsabers, and I'm not sure why, but I owned four of them and always had them in my car. Since Adam associated me with the instrumentals, I started listening to techno a lot since it was about sound and had nothing to do with vocals. Employed for two years with *RadioShack*, I was told that I had the ability to become a store manager, but first, I had to go to an M.I.T. course.

Lee and I were on our way to *West Nanuet* to this "Manager In Training" class when my car started to overheat, so I called my boss; Lee contacted his boss, and we informed them that we were not going to make it to our destination. While I contacted roadside assistance, my iPod started playing a *Star Wars* techno beat. Lee and I looked at each other, seized the sabers from the back of my car and started to duel on the side of the *Taconic State Parkway* with two 12-inch subwoofers and a 750-watt amp bumping in the trunk! We were boisterous, and people were cheering and honking as they passed us. Lee's boss called me and said, *"I can't believe you're both playing with lightsabers!"* I expressed to *"Samsonite"* that I wasn't going to be dismayed about my car, and because I was not making it to the meeting, I wanted to rejoice by clashing sabers with Lee. Samsonite chuckled, and we ended the phone call.

Once the car engine simmered down, Lee and I chuckled about the circumstance towards his house, but the laughter would redirect on yours truly. Lee and I entered his home and played *Yu-Gi-Oh* in the living room, and my blood sugar started to drop; so, he told me that I knew where to go in the kitchen to obtain my requirements, so I helped myself and in minutes, plunged to the ground. I went to open this cupboard, and it wouldn't budge, so I tugged and tugged, and an unforeseen horseshoe about two feet above my head, wedged between the two door handles on the cabinet above the cupboard; to keep it shut just descended on my head, cracking my head open. Lee sprinted to the kitchen and laughed because all he heard was moaning from the next room after the clanking sound. He commented that the horseshoe had never moved from that location for as long as he had been living there, so I began laughing and retorted, *"I wish we were at the meeting because this would've been avoided,"* and we finished the night playing cards until one in the morning!

A couple of months later, my boss was departing from this store, and his replacement was a young fellow named John who was great with customers but had an ego issue, and for me knowing how I was, our worlds would collide if he were drunk with power because I too had an immense ego since I was running operations prior to his arrival. I worked at *Dunkin Donuts* in the morning and *RadioShack* in the afternoon. I was wired on caffeine every time I came to

RadioShack, but crazy enough, a co-worker introduced me to energy drinks, something I did not need. My blood sugar was dropping, and I told John, *"I'll be right back. I'm going across to GNC to get a Red Bull."* He replied, *"No, you're not! You're staying right here!"* Furthermore, he told my fellow employees not to get me a Red Bull, and then Silva questioned who I was contacting when he saw me pick up the store phone, and I stated, *"I'm calling reinforcement because John will not deny me sugar while my glucose is dropping."* I called *RadioShack*, where Michael worked, and Silva questioned, *"You're calling your brother? Ohhh man!"* and chuckled about it. Michael spoke to his boss and said to me on the phone, *"Bro, I told my boss I need to take care of some business. I'm heading towards you, and I'll grab you a Red Bull!"*

While John was in the back office, he had no idea about what had just occurred, but the employees were engaged in the hype and ready to see the collision of management, and the unity in brotherly bond, and I had the upper hand with Michael, a Marine on my side! My brother arrived at the mall in fifteen minutes, and when he approached the store with his military vest, Michael's face had intensity written on it, while my boss looked timid once stepping back onto the sales floor from the back office. As Michael turned into the store, it reminded me of *The Terminator* scene at the mall when the *T-800* robot came to protect what he was programmed to shield from the *T-1000*, and Michael came to my aide when I needed support! Michael passed me the Red Bull, and I drank it quickly and stated that I'd be better within minutes. Michael vocalized to me that if I needed anything, to give him a call, and I proceeded to thank him. Feeling empowered by the brotherly bond with Michael's backup, I soaked it in, and my boss couldn't do a thing to stop the assistance! Once Michael left the premises, John approached me and uttered that he didn't know my blood sugar was dropping, which I perceived as a lie.

The relationship between him and I would change as time progressed, and we strove to prove who was better in sales as management egos clashed. Everything was tending to my favor because I was gaining the likes of people, friends were relying on me, customers returned to work with me, and I was getting the recognition I sought to achieve, and this was *what I wanted*! The District Manager acknowledged me as *"Employee of the month"* for selling the most cell phones during this period. I felt very accomplished as everything was going well, but during this time, George and Kristie were relocating, which stung because I hung out with George every Friday and or Saturday when I was available, and our fun as neighbors were coming to an end! An ex from *Oasis* would enter my work grounds with a saddened expression to inform me that Jermaine had passed into the next realm! I saw him about two weeks prior, and we had planned to hangout on his birthday. He was staying in a shelter about thirty minutes south of my location and wondering why he didn't contact me; the truth was that Jermaine was stabbed by two low-lives on his 20th birthday! I was in a state of shock as my eyes fluttered with tears, and a photo of Jermaine and I was inserted in the newspaper, and it was at that moment I acknowledged that I had lost more than a friend but a dear brother!

Three months later, I started dating a young gal who I met at the bowling alley. We'd follow each other to the concession stand surreptitiously and would eventually exchange numbers. She was absolutely breathtaking in her visage, and we began dating the last week of June, and Stephanie was thrilled to introduce me to her mother. Stephanie's mom owned many horses, and I thought this was gratifying because I always wanted to date a *"Cowgirl"* per se! What I enjoyed about this new experience was being shown how to ride horseback, and Steph stated over the phone that she wanted to meet my dad, and if he were willing to ride a horse, she'd show him the ropes.

I expressed to my dad that I was going to Stephanie's barn to hang out with her and the family, and my father never trotted on a horse, so he was excited to tag along when I asked if he'd like to meet them. Once we arrived, he was enthralled by the real-life setting, and I requested the family not to inquire about cigarettes since I believe my dad had no knowledge of me smoking during this time! I did not know how the new character of my dad would react, and since I wasn't close to him, I didn't want to hear criticism or be embarrassed. I told myself that he was in the same league as before, just playing for a different and victorious team now, so I had to have an open mind about it! Seeing Dad on a horse was an amazing sight, and he had an entertaining experience. I concluded that my father was simply practicing moral excellence as he relinquished his former self with the renewing of his mind! Romans 12:12 says, "And do not be conformed to this world, but be transformed by the renewing of your mind, so that you may prove what the will of God is, that which is good and acceptable and perfect."

Stephanie and I went moonlight bowling every Friday for some time, and it was always a treat doing anything with her, but on this one particular evening, we were positioned to the left side of some people who are classified as "low life" and I was not exactly a fan of theirs because of how they represented themselves. One of these hood rats was eye-balling Stephanie, and I had a major problem with that because his demeanor was so low; he looked to be the type to plot a malicious act just to prove a point, and I didn't trust him! When Stephanie and I would knock down all the pins for a strike, we would give each other a high-five or a kiss and one of these goof balls grew aggravated as his body language spoke volumes. He eventually uttered something after I picked up the bowling ball, and before I threw it, I said, *"We're here to have a good time! Ain't nobody fighting with anybody!"* I watched my bowling ball knock down all ten pins, and when I turned around, I didn't receive a kiss or a high-five but rather a punch to my nose by this jerk's associate who was more than double my weight and almost a foot taller than me. I freaking hate bullies! As I got up from the floor with a bloody nose, the assaulter began running with some of his crew, and I ran after them, but by the time I got outside, they were jumping in a jeep that was already waiting for them. The police were called, of course, and a report was written and filed. The assaulter's family told the police that they had no idea what happened or what I was talking about, which caused an angered expression to develop on my face, but in the end, it didn't change the fact that Stephanie was leaving the bowling alley the same way she came in, and that was with me, not him!

Stephanie and her mother would visit me at *RadioShack*, and it was ideal for me to receive those visits because when I needed lifting, she always arrived at that precise moment when it was required! My boss was getting transferred, and I was getting relocated to Samsonite's store, and since I was demoted because of this relocation, I cared little for the protocol since my tier dropped, and I knew I was better than just a sales associate! Months later, I came into work questioning associates about where the boss was, and the response given was that he did not show up to work and nobody knows his whereabouts. I knew something was not right, and when the District Manager entered the store, he sauntered into the back office and, in minutes, reprimanded me because none of Samsonite's paperwork was organized. I expressed to him that it was not my office, I was not the Assistant Manager, nor was it my responsibility!

Getting bellowed for someone else not doing their job is a pet peeve, especially if I'm not in charge! The District Manager was about to express his final statement towards me, but before he could, Samsonite called my cellphone, and I was wearing a Bluetooth and answered, being ready to be relieved of my duties. Samsonite heard what was transpiring and told me not to mention that he was on my phone. The DM couldn't believe that I answered my phone during his termination rant. I informed him that I was done with *RadioShack,* and he shouted, *"You're Fired!"* Samsonite said that he was working at a cell phone kiosk by the *Palisades Mall,* and Nextel's were the hottest commodity trending, and everybody wanted to have the ring back tones on their phones, so Samsonite informed me to work with him. I agreed to follow up with Samsonite post-day since this was a money-making opportunity!

I was fixed on earning my finances and strove for nothing less than to accomplish this task. I proceeded toward the kiosk at the mall and began my training. The product knowledge was easy to obtain, and by the end of the evening, I knew the ins and outs of my job description at this kiosk. Samsonite asked as we exited the mall, *"What's the best way to get back home?"* I punched my address into my GPS, and as we headed south bound on the Parkway, I saw Samsonite's car fly by me, so I naturally started accelerating. He called my cellphone to state that the vehicle that passed me was not him, so I looked in my rear-view mirror and saw his car after counting the vehicles, and that's all it took for the damage to unfold. When I looked ahead, a licensed driver was trying to make an illegal *"U"* turn on the highway, and then I T-boned her vehicle. She was a deer to headlights; I couldn't stop, and once this collision occurred, my airbags deployed and knocked me incoherent for a few seconds, and a young girl shouted, *"We killed him!"* Although I was stunned, this didn't mean I became deaf! The older woman was so fearful or drunk that she attempted to leave the scene of the accident and, in the process, hit two more vehicles behind me. I remember hearing Samsonite shouting, *"Steve! Steve! Wake up bro!"* He grabbed my phone and called my house, and I believe Desiree picked up the phone when Samsonite called. The impact was so extreme that it literally made my Neon look like a Volkswagen bug. My parents were informed of where I would be transported, and once everything was completed, I arrived at my house with my parents around three or four in the morning. Later that afternoon, someone dropped me off at Stephanie's house, and since my car was totaled, I stayed at her abode for a month, had my game systems, went bowling every Friday, and could horseback ride whenever I wanted with Stephanie, so there was no complaining from me.

The customer service milieu was my forte, whereas labor work was not my cup of tea! I would sleep in most mornings and proceed to walk over to the barn for maybe an hour or so to clean stalls, saddles or even drop off the green hays to the horses before quickly returning back to the house to play *"Shadow The Hedgehog"* with Stephanie's younger sister. I worked almost every day between multiple jobs for years, so to have the freedom of not working an 8-hour day… wow, what a peaceful perception… or so I thought! I guess gaming was an addiction, and it ended my relationship only thirty days after staying at Steph's home. Her mother walked into their home and said, *"Get your stuff and leave!"* Stephanie was no longer feeling effusive about the relationship, and a bowling friend stated, *"I bet Steph's sister said something because she's been flipping out all day, and you did nothing wrong, Steve!"*

The guy in the room would be the individual driving me home, and it meant a lot to hear a positive note after a negative moment, but the wolf was wearing sheep skin as it was only a matter of time before he dated Stephanie, and this was a kick in the shin for me. Talk about being distraught, and all I heard in my head was, *"You don't realize how much you love something until it's gone,"* It was painful to accept such a forfeiture! I wish I had given more of myself to Stephanie versus playing video games, but I didn't, and this game was now over and became a one-way attraction! Stephanie began making fun of my physique and grew ice-cold toward me. Sean supported me and told me to remain strong because I could do without her. The scars that hurt the most were the ones that others could not see, and this pain was suppressed on top of other bottled-up distress!

A couple of months after the relationship with Stephanie concluded, I began dating *"Barbz."* While it is not okay to judge people, I should've used my judgment, and instead, I followed my heart which was born with deceit! A slight mental tug of war would occur as some said it was ill-advised to date Barbz, whereas others disagreed with those individuals. This relationship was fabricated because it was based on lustful desires! During this time, my employer was *MACY'S*, and I was working with both Jerry and Lee. Another friend who also worked at the mall told me, *"Steve, I gave her a concussion once, and I have no problem knocking her out again if she hurts you!"* Jaclyn and I have this brother-sister bond that can never be broken or replaced! Barbz was very hospitable, always providing my favorite foods and letting me watch wrestling or entertain her younger brother with my video games. Barbz's mother referred me to work at a bank. I enjoyed the six-month experience, but it wasn't for me. Since my Neon was totaled in that accident, my mom was kind enough to let me drive the minivan to transport myself from Point A to wherever. The cool thing about the van was that it had no backseats, so I hooked it up, and it became the lounge on wheels.

I had pillows, blankets, and a portable seven-inch screen, and I connected my GameCube console to enable my ability to play *Shadow*. It was great being the older brother to those younger than me; any time they needed me, I was there to assist. Adam and *"E"* became my best friends, and after work, I would pick them up, get a cheap bottle of blue hypnotic and head to the *Palisades Mall* for *Dave & Busters*. This was every Monday for six months, and just to be clear, I was not drinking and driving but did consume in the parking lot, so we could be somewhat numb but not dumb, not drunk and enjoyed playing games. I smoked herbs as it made me more attentive, whereas others might get paranoid. I made sure that my younger brothers were home between 8 and 8:30 p.m. so I could watch wrestling by 9 o'clock! Around this period, I was like a kingpin, and nobody messed with me, and with that said, my new alias became *"Shadow"* to some, although the majority of people still addressed me as *LILROCK*. I was on great terms with the security guards at the mall, as well as the security at the *Town Center*, so nobody ever bothered me because I was acquaintances with them all! It was statistically proven that when people were in my circle, they did not get into trouble, but I can't say the same if I was in theirs. I usually handled situations professionally if one would arise and always felt like an advocate or the voice to the silent. I was often in a suit and ready to take a stand to defend others when they required assistance!

Months down the line, Jerry was now working at *Sears*, the other mall anchor store, in the loss prevention department. I received a phone call from him as he questioned my whereabouts since he noticed through the security footage that my girl was with Duane and holding "Pistachio's" hand! I rancorously sauntered towards *Sears* when I saw the three of them on the ground floor and grew angrier. I've always been faithful to my loyalty, and it was clear that none of them cared for my friendship! Barbz asked, *"Steve, can we go outside and talk?"* I agreed, and when we made our exit, she locked her eyes on my furious, raged pupils and pulled the *"I'm pregnant"* card! I asked if she was serious, and she stated that she was not lying. I grabbed her by her waist and lifted her up with struck excitement. She reentered the mall, and with a thoughtful look with both hands placed on my hips, I professed, *"This isn't my kid,"* with a heavy sigh, my head shifted downward, and it dawned on me why some instructed me to reject Barbz in the first place since there's no loyalty! Duane sent me a text saying that Barbz instructed him to lie to the police and agree that he witnessed me slam her on the ground but told me that he was not going to defend her lie! The mall cop approached me outside of my vehicle and questioned, *"Steve, your girlfriend told me you slammed her on the ground and have a knife?"* I explained what occurred, and he stated that the other officers could see right through her lies, so with a convoluted tale, the police did not believe her, and the officer instructed me to just leave, not stress this and to have a good night!

I started my car and elevated the volume to the song *"Poison"* to remind myself that this was exactly what Barbz had become to me, and I needed to get rid of this toxic as she proved herself unworthy of dating me. Moments later, the police called my parents' home asking for me, and Barbz slandered me so much that she now got my parents involved. I received a phone call from my mother in a concerned tone that the police were scouting for me. We exchanged some words, and it ended with heat. I informed her that I would be staying at Danielle's house and would not be coming home! Barbz and I ended our relationship. I was thrilled about this because I found out that she had relations with two guys on our year anniversary while I was inside her house playing video games with her little brother! I realized that I could, in fact, live with this loss because I would hope to gain someone worth having, and Cristie would be dating me days later! The steps I chose following my drive to Danielle's residence were very foolish, and I was internally boiling and slipped into a moment of darkness. As soon as I walked into Danielle's place, I saw someone drinking *99 Apples*. I never drank it before and got drunk quickly and not on purpose but because I don't drink. All the people in this house were concerned for me because of my diabetes, and they all looked out for me. We were all misguided, but we did care about each other!

After all this chaos occurred with Barbz, more dreadful things would be approaching my direction because it wasn't exactly resolved. I had personal belongings inside Barbz's house, and my items were taken to the police station by her mother, and my parents went to claim my property. Children do not elaborate on many things in life to their parents, and I was one of those young adults that weren't close to mine, so what was exchanged in speech was limited. The mother of the opposing family informed my parents acrimoniously about the time she walked in on Barbz and me having sex. I felt like I was being judged for old news, which her mother was okay with then! I'm not one to boast about such mannerisms, and now that this rabbit was pulled from the hat, I felt embarrassed.

My parents at no time discussed the birds and the bees with me growing up, so this was very uncomfortable once I knew they were aware of my sin. Barbz's mother never had an issue with what she observed transpiring in her daughter's bedroom because she walked away only to return seconds later and began blowing bubbles! If anyone tries to embarrass me in front of my friends or family, they're asking for a discordant verbal confrontation from me, and I won't back down. Not one iniquity is greater than another, so to be realistic, people shouldn't judge others because their sin is different than their own, but most do, and her mother did! Once this conflict between Barbz and I was finalized, Cristie and I were ready to have a brawl with Barbz and her people. I was my squad leader and felt very empowered as we all gathered in a parking lot and looked like a pentad of troublemakers ready to start pandemonium. The police drove by slowly on multiple occasions within a short period and both groups casually left the area! Since Barbz could always go to the mall and bother me if she chose to do so, *what I wanted* was to not work at *MACY'S* since my job was close to her residence.

I obtained an occupation at *Applebee's* and worked my way to closing supervisor, doing what I enjoy doing, taking charge, and serving customers! Working at *Applebee's* was great because it allowed me to interact and serve many tables simultaneously and show my skills. The hiring manager was a jerk because he told me there was a drug screening and implied that I would not pass. I told him this poses no problem, and he said, *"But it's a mouth swab, not a urine sample."* The manager called me a week later and said to come in for training, and upon my arrival, he specified, *"I didn't think you were going to pass, but I'm glad that you did!"* I was insulted that he would make such a statement because I felt like he was implying that I smoke marijuana because I'm Hispanic, but I wasn't worried since I was ready to prove to him my talents. There's only one person that I strive to be better than on this planet, and that's who I was yesterday, and this is no easy walk.

What I enjoyed the most about my job was working for my hard-earned tips, and the paycheck was a bonus! An elderly gentleman and his grandson came to dine-in and appreciated the service so much that he handed me a Benjamin on a $38 check and said, *"Keep the change!"* I showed my boss Lulu, and she was very impressed, as was I, and there were coworkers serving for hours, and on this single table, I received more tips than they did their whole shift. My role when working is to show that I'm the best at what I do, and when it comes to learning anything new, it is always difficult before it gets easier, but working with people was nothing new for me, so this customer service was easily venerated! I realized at this moment that I was not created to fit in because I was created to stand out! One of the guys in the kitchen heard about my tip, elevated his voice, and said, *"LILROCK G-5 XCLUSIVE Gettin' Money!"* No matter how you sliced it, I was addressed as *LILROCK* or *G-5* at *Applebee's* by the kitchen staff, who all respected me, and I in return valued them.

As a closing supervisor, I had to make sure I was on top of everything, including having all the wait staff's telephone numbers for coverage, but a jealous boyfriend of a coworker with whom I went to high school basically threatened me for having his girlfriend's Nextel number. In my opinion, he made his own music, which was terrible; he thought he was God's creation to all but was nothing more than a low-life narcissist who sold garbage rap music on the street! *"Kay"* knew that I didn't like her like that, and she was aware of my loyalty to Cristie, but if Kay's boyfriend commanded her to do something, she wouldn't hesitate even if she knew he was wrong.

So, there was an afternoon when I was hanging out with two women who were best friends and were seated in their car while drinking alcohol before they went to see a movie at the *Town Center*. Jean told me to sit on her lap with my legs stretched over her friend's lap. I saw nothing wrong with the innocence of this act as we are friends and complied. I'm pretty convinced that Jean was lesbian anyway, but I could be wrong. Once I settled into the vehicle, I was handed a bottle of Old English in my left hand and began sipping it despite not being a fan of alcohol. As I was leaning back with the bottle, I had a cigarette in my right and felt untouchably tranquil, and of course, there's always one to ruin another's enjoyment. I caught a hard punch from Kay's boyfriend behind my head from the passenger window, and I wasn't about to let this hood rat get away from this hit-and-run. He started running his mouth, so I politely asked Jean to hold the bottle, slid across her friend's lap and out the driver's door.

After exchanging some words, he had a member of his posse approach me and stare me down, and once we locked eyes, my feet were planted, and he punched me in the face. My head turned to a nine o'clock angle, and as I slowly turned my face towards him, I expressed that I'll give him to the count of five to run before I go take Jean's crowbar and do damage. The leader of this pack shouted,

"*Bro, let's go!*" and as I noticed him with a fast pace towards a car, the driver was Kay, and she looked ashamed for what she allowed to occur and was guilty by association! After this assault occurred, our friendship never fashioned itself to what it was prior and I never saw his face again!

Devoted to my loyalty, Cristie and I were now more often together than not, had many of the same friends, played video games and usually had fun. She's a drinker, and again, that was not my cup of tea, but she controlled herself for the most part, and I was never embarrassed around her when she consumed because she rarely acted like she was a couple of olives short of a martini when drinking. I was in the *Town Center* one evening by *McDonald's*, meeting a few friends after work, when Duane and Pistachio approached me, and Pistachio initiated talking negatively about his girlfriend like that was supposed to put us on respectable terms. My friends and I were not trying to engage in this conversation, so we used body language to express to each other that we were ready to depart from this location and head to Danielle's house to have a party! We all arrived at Danielle's place, parked our vehicles, and entered her home, and the night was expected to be a blast. Approximately ten minutes later, I walked back to my car to retrieve the video game I had left behind, and once in the proximity of the vehicle, I clenched my right fist and instantly became motionless! Not only did those two jerk wads follow me without my notice, but one or both slashed two tires on the van.

I was so disturbed that I smoked pot as an excuse to keep calm and was reacting to my feelings as opposed to observing who my peers were and what they did for a living. The two guys who lived in this household were mechanics and assisted me with this ordeal, and another person at this gathering was a tow truck driver as well. I was aligned with the right individuals at this time but had the wrong attitude, and who could blame me? I was, however, fortunate not to have work the next two days, so these two mechanics were able to acquire the proper tires and put them on to get me rolling. I felt like a ticking time bomb waiting to detonate and really had no concept of peace! Tick-Tock!

Since I was temporarily staying here after that kerfuffle with my mother, I took my portable television, GameCube console and my PlayStation games out of the van and inside Danielle's residence. Four individuals lived here; Danielle and her boyfriend Ceccil, who were the two I trusted, and his brother *"Seth"* and his girlfriend. A week later, Cristie and I were headed towards Danielle's place after my work shift had concluded, and I was excited to relax after having a great workday. This was another highlighted evening shift where a customer came in with his wife, collectively had a bill of $87, and the gentleman handed me $150 and stated to have a goodnight! I was astonished yet not surprised because everything was balanced perfectly with these guests!

Cristie and I arrived at Danielle's house when I inquired Seth about where my items were moved, and he stated that they were robbed! I told him that I was calling the police, and he frantically said, *"LILROCK, I got this. Please don't call the police!"* Cristie and I turned around, left the premises, and never returned to this home. Danielle informed me that she discovered from Ceccil that my stuff was exchanged for drugs. Cristie abruptly stated that she absolutely knew that this *"scumbag"* had taken my items, her words, not mine! As time progressed, I remained growing a hard heart! We both knew that I was saturated with anger and no woman wants to be involved with a mad man, yet Cristie remained. When I thought things couldn't get any worse, of course, they did! I was working an evening shift when I was going to drive a few coworkers home, and as we were leaving the job, one of the girls asked, *"Can I pull up the car?"* I said, *"Sure"* because my glucose was dropping, and I saw no harm in this as I'm thinking that she is only assisting me. I went back inside to get lemonade, and when I walked outside, the damage was done! She crashed into a brand-new parked car, purchased that morning in mere seconds! I was acrimonious but could blame nobody but myself, and it wasn't even like I said *"Sure"* because I had an affinity towards her because that was definitely not the case. The woman who purchased this Jeep walked outside of *Applebee's* and laughed at what happened but was not rancorous by the situation, which was unexpected. The van was towed, eventually fixed and was operable for a limited time. During the time frame of not having a vehicle, my girl had an attitude, altering her ways, and I was puzzled, which led me to believe that she was using me.

We shrugged off the relationship, which was not *what I wanted*, and she began dating another person immediately, which then began my next chapter!

CHAPTER 7

FOOLISHLY ENTRAPPED TO INCARCERATION

I was attracted to a tall blonde two years older than me who has children, and I noticed her profile on my friend Steven's *"Myspace"* page, and he told me this was his aunt and would arrange a time when she and I could meet and hangout. The first time I physically met her, she was shocked at how short I stood and called me *"mini-me,"* but because she was so eye-catching, this nickname never struck a chord with me! I, in return, called her *"Cinderella"* and would drive to her apartment twice a week to spend the night. The idea that she was *"out of my league"* was just a thought until I gained confidence in my passion for dating her. She accepted me as she observed, and I was super hyped about it! Cinderella was eventually moving, and I was willing to relocate with her, and since my favorite color is blue, she started buying everything that color, from kitchen place mats, belts, shirts, sneakers etc. She owned nothing blue prior, so seeing her do this for me was endearing.

The summer of 2007 started great because I was in a relationship with a gorgeous woman, was financially established as a waiter who was a closing supervisor and was attempting to move out! A going away soiree would be established for myself and two others by Cristie and her friend Matt at his home. It was nice to have no friction with her since Cinderella was where I had my happiness, and I cared for her immeasurably.

Jon contacted me days later, stating that he needed a place to stay and requested a ride to Pistachio's house. I was very reluctant to do this favor, but Jon and I were on a six-year friendship, and because I enjoyed being "the brother" to many, I honored his favor despite him going through whatever weird phase he was walking and despite me wanting to punch Pistachio in the face. Leaving the past in the past, Barbz now reentered my circle again, and as Cristie and I transported Jon, we were welcomed into this home of theirs and came to a consensus to enter but only for a brief period. Cristie and I had plans to hang out with Matt, which was why she was with me. Barbz owned a kitten that was very petite. Its bowl with the milk was bigger than the creature itself, and Pistachio didn't care for this kitten, had trust issues with Barbz and was apparently hooked on sniffing the white rock!

Pistachio specified to me that he no longer wanted the kitten as a result of expenses. I took the idea into consideration and proceeded to leave with Cristie. The following afternoon, Jon invited me to go to a *Buddhist Monastery* with Barbz and Pistachio. I was curious as to what I may observe since I've never stepped foot on these grounds, so they picked me up, and we went about our expedition! Upon our arrival, there was a sense of peace since there was no chaos, but this peace did not reside with me and began casting a dark cloud over us, metaphorically and literally. I observed a cluster of grown men idolizing a vast statue and questioned, *"Can we leave, or were we supposed to see something special today?"* As the experience ended, Jon noticed a jade dragon in the shape of a boat positioned by a wishing fountain. Barbz, Pistachio and I approached the vehicle, entered the car, and began rolling towards the exiting gate when suddenly Jon dashed like a bullet and said frantically, *"Go, go, go!"* He snagged the dragon from its position and then handed it to me, thinking I could use it for something, but it became nothing more than a temporary décor for my bedroom, and all I did was hope that Karma wouldn't kick me in the rear for the act of another without my demand for the item!

Sometime after the trip to the *Buddhist Monastery*, Barbz and Pistachio were evicted and resided at his mother's home. Pistachio verbalized to me that he knew Cristie wanted the kitten because she apparently uttered that inside the home of his former residence. One week later, the minivan died, and I fretted a little about how I would transport myself to work! Pistachio hollered at me from his mother's home phone and told me that the kitten was inside, ready for pick up! He stated that he would leave the front door unlocked so the animal could be retrieved. I called Danielle, and she picked up Cristie and then me, and we proceeded to Pistachio's location. When we arrived, the front door was locked. As Danielle and Cristie remained in the car, I went about calling Pistachio, and he stated that his mother locked the door but not to worry because around the corner of the house was an open window and in that room was where the kitten was to be found. I reached in to grab the kitten, but because of my short stature, I fell through the window, grabbed the kitten, casually walked out the front door, jumped into Danielle's car, and left. Cristie and I were dropped off at our respective addresses, and later that evening, both were picked up by Danielle and proceeded to Matt's house.

Matt had to work an overnight inventory shift for the store he managed, which left Cristie and me alone this Monday evening. I recall us watching wrestling, as this is my favorite weekly episodic television entertainment to view, and once the program concluded, we looked deep into each other's eyes and knew what we desired but resisted since we were not in a relationship with each other. Moments later, Cristie received a phone call from her mother asking why State Troopers arrived at their doorstep for the kitten she brought home! Cristie clarified what had occurred and told her mother where she was after her mom inquired about her location. I then received a frantic phone call from Barbz minutes later saying, *"Steve, I can't give you the kitten because someone stole her!"* I replied, *"What? Ask your boyfriend where the kitten is!"*

She questioned him, and he uttered that he did not know. I knew she didn't want to give up this kitten, so I understood that this was an entrapment. I heard the police dispatching in the background and hastily said, *"I'm on my way to Yonkers. I have to go!"* Cristie and I calmly freaked out and sought out a plan. We proceeded to abscond the basement and head upstairs to wait for Cristie's mother to arrive, and since Matt was working, the police could not enter his home without permission! Cristie called Matt to inform him of what was happening since he was the individual who was going to drive us both home that evening. We both pulled the window blinds to peak outdoors when she said, *"My mom is here. I have to go!"* I was frozen by movement because I knew in the core of my body that something bad was going to happen, and seconds later, the police were right behind her mother's vehicle. Cristie and I hugged each other tightly and said bye, and she stated, *"I will tell them that you left!"* As she left the premises, all I said in my brain was that I couldn't believe that she was about to get arrested. She started waltzing down the driveway, was handcuffed immediately and placed in the State Troopers' vehicle. As soon as they started moving, Matt flew in front of the police car and into his driveway, and when I viewed this, my blood sugar started elevating rapidly, and I began to feel very fatigued with anxiety.

Observing the perimeter and questioning where I was going to conceal myself, I headed towards Matt's sisters' room but felt like I would be violating her privacy if I entered her closed bedroom door. I worked with her at *Applebee's* and did not want to see anything my eyes were not supposed to view. Matt provided the police access into his home, and I needed to dash somewhere and could not believe this was happening and thought to myself that this nut job Pistachio really set me up! I should have used better judgment and now I'm pissed! I exponentially bolted up the stairs and wanted to hide underneath a bed, but unluckily there were boxes from corner to corner, and not even my small frame could fit in this diminutive area. The cops secured the entire house except for the attic as I heard the police dispatch on their radio that both levels of the house were cleared.

I exhaled a sigh of release, and then Matt *"Alerted"* my Nextel for some inexplicable imprudent reason, and a police officer started marching up the stairs as they heard the bleep to my Nextel. The female trooper said, *"Hmmm, look what we have here!"* I sat on the bed with my hands folded on my lap and expressed, *"I'm not resisting arrest, but can you tell me what I'm being charged with?"* She told me that she would be asking the questions. I was escorted out of the home with metal bracelets around my wrist and positioned in the back of a different vehicle than Cristie. I could not believe that I was detained for something that was entrapment, but I really should have known better! My glucose level elevated to a number that demanded an ambulance to aid me to an emergency room, but this putrid attitude of an officer denied me! Once I was led to the police barracks, I was shackled to a wall by my legs. Cristie was in the interrogation room solo and throwing a fit because the man she cared about was about to die outside the cross-examination area. I informed the police that I was not well, and unless they wanted me to puke on their floor, they needed to release me from these chains!

As time progressed, my Nextel phone died, and post mugshot, the female trooper exchanged my dead battery with hers to look at who I was communicating with earlier that day. I felt very violated by this woman for many reasons, and her lust for power persona royally stank! Interrogated individually, Cristie and I explained to the department what occurred from beginning to end and both stories aligned with each other. The interrogator questioned who Cinderella and Danielle were, and I replied that one was my girlfriend and the other my sister, not a blood relation, but my sister nonetheless! She proceeded to contact Danielle and told her to come in for questioning.

Hours passed, and it was around six a.m. when I heard the train passing through town, and coursing through my mind was that my parents were leaving that train station to attend their occupation and had no idea that I was roughly one thousand feet from the platform. Cristie shouted to the police, *"Give him his insulin. He's a diabetic, you effing animals!"* When she said this, Cristie didn't censor her mouth, and she fought hard for me. Two male troopers were exchanging words with each other when one of them said, *"I remember him; he's the person with diabetes that was doing seventy in the thirty, going to the gas station because his sugar was dropping."* I was amazed that they remembered that evening with me because that was five years prior to this occurrence, but I guess I have one of those faces that people can simply remember. I was pale and very fatigue and stated to this nasty woman that it was vital that she stop playing with my life and have someone check my blood sugar, but it didn't matter what I needed. She wasn't willing to comply until after the interrogation or after I was motionless. She should have been indefinitely dismissed from her job duties for not serving and protecting, as that is what the police are supposed to do, and some officers like her don't, which is unfortunate!

Once the investigation was completed, the medical team arrived, checked my blood sugar, and stated that I needed to be taken to the hospital urgently because my glucose was 938! This poor excuse of a woman abruptly said, *"No, you give him insulin now because he's going to jail!"* Facing downward, chained to the wall with my hands folded, I slowly elevated my head, gulped, and replied, *"I'm going where?"* I suddenly felt like my world shattered since I would now have a police record for the nonsense of another, and I felt victimized! I was *foolishly entrapped to incarceration,* and it turned out that Pistachio felt threatened and needed me out of her circle because there was no hostility from me towards Barbz. I was not willing to remain infuriated about my past to miss out on my present, but Pistachio struck me in a way where I could not retaliate... yet! I was now being charged with second-degree burglary, petit larceny, and criminal trespassing in the second degree. Cinderella had a birthday coming up in a couple of weeks, and I didn't know if I was going to see her. I asked a male officer if I could use the phone to call my boss, and the policeman allowed me to do so before departing to *Valhalla*. I called my supervisor and asked if I could be removed from the schedule, elaborating to Lulu that I was going to jail!

She asked why, and when I elucidated the situation, Lulu chuckled and replied, *"Steven, when you get out, just call me, and I'll put you on the schedule that evening."* Let me just say that I was grateful not to have to forfeit my job and was blessed with an awesome boss! I went to the courthouse to see the judge and then was sent to booking, but having my sugar level at almost a thousand and not knowing what to expect next didn't allow me to be in the right state of mind, nor could I be since I was physically drained and mentally broken. People who have a police record will say that a week in jail is peanuts, but to someone like me who has never been arrested or locked up, this was devastating, especially since I didn't know at this particular time the length of my incarceration. Tick-Tock!

Upon entering the jail compound, I was put in a holding cell and was excited to see a phone. I called my house, but the landline did not accept collect calls, so I called Cinderella, but she didn't pick up. I didn't need to have someone put money on a prepaid call for me to get a message delivered because when I called from the jail, the greeting would say, *"State your name!"* I would give a message instead of my name so the person I was calling would hear my message, followed by *"An inmate from Westchester County Jail is placing a collect call. Do you wish to accept?"* Once I was released from this location, I became uncomfortable because the first thing required of me was being coerced to strip naked, bend my knees and cough in front of this overgrown man. Once I completed stripping down, I was given this big vest that dropped just passed my knees and keep in mind that I am just under 5 feet and felt humiliated! I saw people that I knew, and they were overjoyed to see me. I didn't think I was tough; I wasn't convinced that I was a criminal, and I wasn't exactly jolly hearing, *"I can't believe Little Rock is here. That's what's up!"* As I walked by the holding cells with the guard, it was written on my face that I was beyond depressed, plus my blood sugar was still high, so I felt disgusted. *"You don't realize how much you love something until it's gone"* was once again meandering in the back of my mind. I was told to enter the cell in the corner of this area, and I sank into deeper hopelessness as I walked in with my head down. The toilet was there with no privacy, it was dark, and I curled up on the cold floor, tearing my eyes out in silence because I was in a foreign environment, out of my element and felt captive because I was locked up and felt forsaken. I was in a realm that was not built for me and was physically, mentally and emotionally unstable.

I came to find out that I was in *"Suicide Watch"* and was offered a bologna sandwich from the guard, and although I'm not a fan of this meat, I ate what was provided despite it tasting awful, and it really was awful. Hours later, I was transferred to the infirmary, and it was as if I was in *Montefiore* hospital again because I entered a room with three men around my age who had a television, and landline phones, were playing cards together and were getting fed the good food. I started feeling better already because I wasn't eating a bologna sandwich and was not alone, but this would be short-lived.

As I was getting comfortable, these guys were providing me with a lot of encouragement, and once my blood sugar was regulated, I was transferred to my permanent cell block until my release date. Scoping the perimeter as I was walking with the officer, I noticed I was entering the *"G Block"* and once entering the block. The C.O. said, *"Enter your cell, inmate,"* and I smirked because it was cell number five. As I entered this place of rest, having nothing, I never thought I'd be so happy to see a roll of toilet paper! Once I heard that clanking noise of the door closing behind me, I walked over to the window and saw emptiness outside, and what I saw on the exterior was exactly how I was feeling internally. Seated on a thin cot, which was on a hard frame extended off the wall, I placed my elbows on my knees, folded my hands, looked up and saw a shelf to do pull-ups on, and there was a book at the corner of the shelf, and it just so happened to be the Bible!

The next morning, I woke up at around 6:30 a.m. to the sound of my cell door opening when the Chief Officer stated that the nurse needed me to walk to the infirmary to check my sugar level. When

I showed up, two officers seated across from the nurses' station had questioned, *"What could you have possibly done to be here?"* but inquired curiously since all they saw was a small-statured man, so I gave them the rundown, and they both laughed and told me to not worry about it because it's petty. One of them stated, *"We have officially met the cat burglar,"* and I chuckled about it.

They stated that the judge would probably throw the case out or give me probation, and once I was done there, I returned to my cell for breakfast. I was permitted to have visitors, and Cristie was there with our friend *"Feder-alley."* This was his nickname because he looked like your typical television undercover cop with the goatee, clothes, speech… the whole nine yards! Prior to entering the visitation room, I was obligated to go through the process of, once again, stripping naked, coughing while squatting, lifting my tongue up and down to show I was concealing nothing in my mouth, and after this procedure was completed, I was granted access to this room. *"Feder-alley"* informed me that Danielle was incapable of coming inside because the visitation limit was two people per inmate.

As Cristie sat in front of me, her eyes flooded with tears, she grabbed both of my hands and said, *"We're going to do our best to get you out of here!"* I practically fell in love with her all over again because of the compassion I witnessed, and her body language spoke volumes, but I knew that I was already reserved for another, and Cinderella was everything to me! During the hour I spent with these two, they complimented me on how well I looked, and they laughed with me when I showed them my pass, which said my name, block, and cell number, so when they saw *"G-5"*, it felt great to smile with those who knew my *"G-5"* nickname. It was miserable observing them leave, but I did value their visit nevertheless!

CHAPTER 8
ROLLER COASTER RIDE

When it came to *"recreation time,"* I didn't know what to do since I didn't know what my options were, and then I noticed someone here that attended middle school with me, and he informed me that I could go outside and play basketball or sit inside and watch television. I told him that I felt like going outside since I was confined to my cell. Prior to going outdoors, one of the guys on this block presented me with brand new shower slippers because I had to wash up at some point, and he told me, *"You do not want to shower barefoot!"* I thought that was honorable, and all I could offer him was my thanks. I continued my walk outside and was the shortest guy on the court playing basketball, but it was great to see that I had a killer three-point shot. I was now becoming what felt like the *"popular guy,"* but only because inmates who were looking outside their cell windows were projecting questions like *"What's your name?", "What are you in for?"* and or *"How tall are you?"* I had to improvise, adapt, and overcome this new environment since I was not homebound in the comfort of my parents' home!

Once I was done with rec time, I went back to my cell, did push-ups and pull-ups, and read the Bible. I was building strength physically but not yet spiritually because I didn't understand much of what I was reading, but God planted a seed of some sort that day, and I knew in my heart that this Bible was here for a reason! As the early dinner was approaching, I needed to walk towards the infirmary to follow up with the nurse for my insulin shot, and as I waltzed through the area, I strolled past the female inmates who were mobile and wearing shackles, and a few of them articulated some words out loud to me that were enjoyable to my ears. Oddly enough, this made me feel delighted, and I received an ego boost because I'm used to women gawking at me from time to time, but I never expected that to happen in jail. Eventually, dinner was served, my workouts were in motion, and reading was set.

The crazy thing about this evening was that while I was scrolling through the scriptures, I came across a verse that said, *"A man's pride will bring him low, but a humble spirit will obtain honor."* God was telling me right here that my ego boost from earlier that day was not from a humbled spirit and must change if I wanted to see a change. By being productive with my time of reading, praying, and thinking, the hours flew, and the next thing I knew, it was lights out on the block!

I was blessed to see another day and wasn't nervous for many reasons. Sure, the food wasn't great, but I was now disciplined to eating three meals a day which regulated my sugars, and I couldn't cheat on my diet because I had no money on my commissary to purchase snacks! In this setting, my blood sugars were stabilized, and I was healthier, gaining weight and becoming more confident! Later that afternoon, I had two visitors and again had to go through the usual protocol before they could see me. I was ecstatic to see my sister Danielle there with *"Feder-alley."* She bought me boxers, t-shirts, a crossword puzzle, and a magazine to read and even put money on my commissary so I could purchase some items for low glucose purposes. She told me not to worry because everything was going to get better, and eventually, I would be out, going to work and seeing my beautiful girlfriend! Danielle has always provided much comfort for me and has never let me down! I eventually went back to my cell to work out, do some crossword puzzles and have some quiet time, which gave me a sense of joy.

Two hours later, another visitor came to greet me with their presence, and this time it was my attorney! I provided the minutiae of the entire situation to him. He retorted with the rundown on what would happen in the courthouse and stated that I would be released Monday because the authorities had no heavy substance of evidence on me. I felt illegally captive but knew this rabbit was going to hop out of the hat and disappear from this place. When Sunday approached, I attended a church service, and to witness this godly man, an outside source, talking about *Thee Source*, which simply paved the way for attentiveness during this hour of listening about this God that loves me! Later that day, it turned out that I had three visitors, but it was unfortunate that I was incapable of seeing either party because of folks acting out of order outside of the facility. Whatever befell out there forced the police to mention to all guests in the waiting line that no one was entering to visit anybody, and I was only entitled to one visitation privilege on this day. I was jubilant that I had less than twenty-four hours until I was released. It turns out that those visitors outside the waiting line were both my parent and Cinderella, yet neither party knew the other.

It's Monday morning, and at six a.m., I'm refreshed, ten pounds heavier and ready to break out of this place. My morning routine was in progress, having my blood sugar checked, eating breakfast, and packing up the clothes Danielle had purchased for me. I couldn't wait to leave this place because not only would I regain my sanity once I was back home, but Cinderella was waiting for me, and work was one of my two main focuses. Since I was feeling healthier and stronger, I was driven to undertake everything my mind was fixed on accomplishing, and as I was getting ready to vacate the premises, I concurrently felt relieved and anxious because my goal was to knockout Pistachio for this entrapment, as he was my other focus!

When I arrived at the courthouse, I immediately noticed Desiree and my mother waiting for me.

The judge called my name and told me that the charges stacked on me would be dropped to a misdemeanor, and I was also given a year of probation. What a small world because you remember Kay from *Applebee's*? Well, it was her mother who was my probation officer. Once I was freed from these hand cuffs, I walked out, and my mother kissed me on top of my head and hugged me. That gentle vibe would be short-lived as I was about to hear negative news that broke my heart in a manner that only made me ignite with rage after drowning in tears, and you can't stop what you can't see coming! Once I entered my mother's vehicle, I was seated in the back, feeling great because I was free, and then Mom asked, *"Who's Cinderella?"* When inquiring, my mother addressed Cinderella's real name, and I replied, *"That's my girlfriend!"* She then questioned, *"You know she has three kids, right?"* As my face darkened, I stated, with a broken, angry tone, *"So what! Single mothers can't be loved?"* She then proceeded to inform me that Cinderella's baby's father called my parents' house and made some sort of threat to my family! My mother didn't have to say anything else about the issue she voiced.

Desiree looked over her left shoulder to see my face fall, and when I lifted my head to gaze at the area from the window, my eyes flooded with tears. Deep down beneath the flesh was a vexed young man who had an unfathomable connection with Cinderella! There was pain underneath this anger, and although disinclined to terminate this relationship, I had to relinquish the affiliation that I enjoyed with her because someone from her end crossed that boundary line that should never be infringed.

Once I returned home, I immediately put my phone on the charger and called my supervisor. Lulu asked with such joy, *"Hey Steven, you're out?"* I told her that I was indeed free from the house of correction, and Lulu replied, *"Great, I'll see you tonight for work!"* I called Cinderella and left a voicemail asking questions about what happened when I was detained. A few hours passed, and I went outside to wait for the arrival of Danielle and Cristie, and when I saw the expressions on their faces when they observed me homebound, it illuminated me because I felt and saw a joyful assembly! Once I attended work, I walked into the back and heard, *"G-5 Xclusive is back,"* and once I heard this articulated from Rome, I felt welcomed with opened arms, and a smile developed on my face.

After explaining to all who asked what occurred, I went about my shift and did what I do best, tend to others and their needs, but once my shift was done, I called Barbz and demanded she tell me Pistachio's location because I was going to break his face and shatter his dreams for setting me up with this entrapment! Barbz told Pistachio that people were coming for him, and he understood that I knew plenty of folks who despised him, and they hated him more for his actions against me! The groups who defended me were not a force to be reckoned with, and Pistachio was going to get what he deserved. Since he caught wind of this information, he committed a crime to get locked up; that way, he was protected! I went to see Cinderella the next day and benignly broke up with her, although I solemnly did not want to but was rendered with no choice. This news deflated her expression, and I needed to be strong and move forward despite how much I wanted to keep her in my life. If people in her lifecycle could operate in such a manner, then that was not an alignment I was willing to have with me on my journey! I wanted to be the best part of Cinderella, but at this point, Cinderella couldn't be the best part of me!

The following morning, I went car shopping with my parents, and they purchased a car for me, I registered it in my name and was excited to drive my own vehicle, and all I could do was offer my thanks to them both for this purchase. It was only a matter of days before I saw Cristie, and we resumed our relationship. I was the closing supervisor at *Applebee's,* and my boss was relocating to a different setting. I enjoyed my profession but had to consider if I really wanted to continue this job during the slow snow days. A new manager would come into position, but he mainly bossed people around and thought he was suave but was nothing more than a nuisance to me. There's a right way to do things in this line of business, and the way this man conducted himself was not going to flow well with me because, as the closing supervisor, I knew how to do my job and didn't need anybody to instruct me on how to perform my duties!

One evening, business traffic started to reduce itself, so we dropped the chart from a seven to a three. Now, only three servers were conducting traffic with the tables to do what we do at our finest. Approximately thirty minutes later, the manager told me, *"Let's drop it down to a three chart."* I alluded to him that this change had already been completed and proceeded to walk over to the two tables that were waiting about five minutes for me to arrive and take their orders. I wrote their entrée desires down and entered them into the P.O.S. system, and after entering the kitchen area, I gathered the beverages for my tables, but the manager demanded I run food out to tables that were not mine. I told him, *"You take them! I've got two tables that I'm currently taking care of, and I need to do this quickly."* I continued my performance, and when he saw me again, he instructed me to go home, and I did not take this news kindly! When I come to work, it's to perform customer service at its best, not slave myself to my boss! We got into a verbal fight, and I knew this was not going to work out, and then the manager said, *"See you tomorrow!"* I didn't see that coming.

The next day I came into work, and he told me to step into the office, and I felt flustered and knew this was over! He told me that yesterday was my last night, and today I'm fired! I cursed him out, then told him, *"You can't fire me. I quit last night after your lazy ass sent me home for doing my job!"* The adrenaline was pumping through my veins, and this appalling *roller coaster ride* made me very ill, elevating my sugar level. I asked myself where I was going to seek employment and aimed for a management position, so I went over to the mall to search for a full-time managerial spot, and after meandering for about twenty minutes, I walked by *Yankee Candle,* which happened to be searching for an Assistant Manager. I walked into the store, asked to speak with the hiring manager, and two weeks later, I was assigned the position. I started mid-November, right before the *Black Friday* season, and it was nice to work under pressure. I had no knowledge about these candles or their accessories but gained enough product knowledge within a short period to prove myself worthy of this position!

One evening, Jon contacted me, and we came to a consensus that I'd stay over his residence for an outdoor Jacuzzi and indoor video game type of night. Jon asked me to invite some friends over, so I called Jaclyn, who brought her friend Vikki, and the four of us had a great time! Once I introduced Jaclyn to Jon, it wasn't long before they started dating, which irked me a little because I had an eye for her, but life continued, and Jon deserved a terrific woman! The next morning when Jon woke up, he walked out of his room and asked, *"Bro, you want to go upstairs and shoot some pool?"* I got off the couch and replied, *"Ok, sounds great!"* When I woke up, I realized my right eye had what appeared to be gunk, and as I tried to get it out, nothing was coming out because this was not an issue with the outside of my eye but rather an internal problem, and this became a major concern.

Later that evening, Cristie and I went to Lens Crafters at the mall to see if I needed glasses or if I could be told what was happening to my eye, but when the lady viewed the scope, she said, *"Oh dear, I'm going to refer you to someone."* I felt another *roller coaster ride* just waiting to flush me with emotional anxiety. Since I had just obtained this new occupation, I was not trying to have my personal life conflict with my profession. Cristie and I started talking about wedding rings and such, and if you know me, you'd know that I always go above and beyond for my lady. I decided to spend over four thousand dollars on an engagement ring with a matching wedding band because I thought she deserved it. I made the purchase at the mall for the convenience of making weekly payments since I work inside the same establishment. Unfortunately, one week later, this jewelry store was filing for chapter eleven, and I was irked because the convenience of making payments in the mall was stripped from being possible.

I asked the sales associate, *"Can I return these?"* He stated that since they were closing, this was not a possibility, but I knew he worked off commission. Some things in life just didn't go as planned, and my responses to many circumstances were not wise. I'm sure the law of attraction had much to do with it because if I was being negative, I ought not to expect anything positive to blossom out of it!

My friend Steven was in the mall, and during this period, he was dating my ex-girlfriend, Kim. Steven commented that I should hang out with them sometime to catch up, and this was not the same

Steven she cheated on me with, so I was okay with his gesture. As I was working, my productivity was not well due to elevated sugars, and I was operating as slow as molasses, the story of my life! I had to set up the store planogram, which was easy, but I felt weak and useless due to my condition. My boss was relying on me to complete the store in the six hours I was working, and if it was not finished, he would have to complete it the following morning and would view the video camera to see why things weren't completed, and this was a bullet I was going to dodge, no question! I called Steven and asked him if he wanted to make twenty dollars, and he responded, *"What do I need to do?"* He walked into the store sometime after and began doing what I needed to finish by the end of this shift.

I was apprehensive about my right eye, and it literally provoked my glucose to boost on a norm, and without checking my sugar levels three times a day minimum, it was easy for my glucose to be off and cause me to be tempered as a side effect. Ha-ha, I guess that was always in my blood. I came in the next day, and my boss *"Paulie"* said, *"Steven, I'm impressed! I question your ability some days, but I was very happy when I walked in this morning."* Since Steven performed so well, Paulie had no reason to review the tape, and I wanted to hire Steven, but we didn't have the budget to employ anybody! This afternoon Kim would drive me to my eye appointment since I would need assistance due to the dilation of my eyes. One day at the doctor's office, it was stated that I was going blind, and I expressed that I could see out of both my eyes and did not comprehend how only one could be salvaged and not the other. I asked the doctor about an eye transplant and was told that this does not exist, and I replied, *"Why don't you just tell me I don't have enough money!"* I was not a fan of this *roller coaster ride*, but when I needed assistance, Kim accommodated me greatly.

I remember Cristie calling me at 4:18 in the morning, asking me to get her chocolate and something sweet because she was encountering her monthly visit and was *"incapable"* of driving. Although I had worked at nine a.m. and slept around midnight, I got dressed, drove twenty minutes away, bought her desires, dropped them off, and drove back home. If she was happy, then I was jovial too, and as her boyfriend, I felt compelled to honor her wishes but began to feel like I was being played in every possible way. If she wanted to borrow my car while I was working, I'd pick her up before work and drop myself off so she could go to class, and if she had no money for food, I'd give her cash when she requested it, and why? I guess I felt that as long as there was a label on us, I had my responsibilities.

I would become argumentative with Cristie when we wouldn't agree on things, and instead of being well-spoken, I would lash out all the time! All she began viewing was my angry behavior, and I knew she would rebel at some point, and she knew she deserved better than what I was providing. The weight of my unhinged rage was weighing me down, and now I was indirectly making her carry my burden with me. The longer I suppressed my emotions, the bigger the mental explosion! I started to vibe that dark hover; when you know something is fishy but can't quite figure it out yet, and the thing is, I cared for this woman and did all that I could for her because it was once expressed to me that if you wait until you can do everything for everybody instead of doing something for somebody, you'll end up doing nothing for nobody! I mentioned earlier about men named *"Steven"*; that they *"may be quick-tempered with those who are not aligned in their manner,"* and with extremely high glucose levels, I was a daily ticking time bomb. Cristie and I were very different, but opposites attract. Although we had our desirability towards each other, we started drifting apart, which plundered me into sadness. I should've been on medication around this time or seeking a therapist. Still, don't confuse my personality with my attitude, my personality is who I am, and my attitude depends on who you are and how well you demonstrate yourself; unless my glucose level is high, then you might just want to stand clear from me! Ritalin would be good right about now.

I enjoyed being in a relationship, but this became a hassle as I grew with rage and needed to find freedom by redirecting my attitude into a positive one. As I continued my position as the Assistant Manager at *Yankee Candle*, I was told that I was needed at the outlet store to cover since the manager had resigned. Upon my arrival, I noticed that these employees were not knowledgeable about the accessories for the merchandise; a gentleman even had a few questions, and the staff responded with, *"I'm not sure."* The employees had no idea who I was, so I intervened and explained why the accessories were beneficial. I introduced myself to the sales representatives, and they were shocked to see that it was I who was the coverage, and since I've been with this company for over a year, I had the product knowledge. Once I met the assistant manager, her body language said that she was agitated about me being in charge and not her! The staff was genuine towards me so that I could be comfortable with them, and one of these ladies was flirting with me a lot, but I wasn't here for anything except business! As the outsider, I'm sure a few of the employees felt like I was a threat to the Assistant Manager whom they love dearly, and perhaps they perceived me as a demon in their sanctuary since I was the outside source invading their turf. In any event, this flirtatious lady started telling me about her boyfriend, and I, in return, elaborated my situation with Cristie. I was an acrimonious person but did not want to portray that character on work grounds and wanted to be a leading friendly boss! Character is a quality that embodies many imperative traits, such as bravery, confidence, perseverance, integrity, and wisdom.

Unlike our fingerprints that we are born with and can't change, character is something that you create from within and must take responsibility for changing. The conversation with this woman developed quite well, and then it became personal. I described the scenario of my arrest with the cat and how I passed the background check because my case was still pending. Foolish me! She and I were locking up the store, and afterward, she expressed to me to come into her car, but I denied her immediately! It would appear that she wanted to mess around, but she was not on my *"to-do"* list! I was here for a few weeks and relished my time being in charge, but the staff was seeking to abolish my reputation, and unfortunately, I delivered them the ingredients! The next day I returned to work at the store I was hired for, and at around eleven a.m., an elderly woman entered and had some questions for me, as did I for her. Once I started to ring her up, she asked me, *"So, what's your favorite scent?"* Once she proposed this question, I knew that she was a *"secret shopper"*, and I failed to ask her that very question but followed everything else that was to be done. When I returned to work the next morning, I felt another dark hover of a cloud in the atmosphere, and even though my boss was quite gentlemanly towards me, I felt like my job was going to slip out of my grasp on this day. I was currently in debt by thousands of dollars, and the extra money would be a great deal of help, so while working in the mall, I searched for another job.

I sought employment at the Halloween store, which Cristie didn't approve of because this store was parallel to her workplace. She, too, had two jobs in the mall, and at her other occupation, I despised her boss with a heavy passion! Adam happened to be at the mall and told me he was not surprised I obtained another job. I saw my girlfriend's manager on the mall premises and decided to confront him since something was off with Cristie, as she was treating me differently. I elaborated on why I had an issue with him face-to-face, and he shoved me, so Adam pushed him back within a flash and said, *"Don't touch him, or I'll knock you where you stand!"* As stated, my people love me and defend me without having to instruct them because that's what real brothers do. This guy was shaken to the core, expressed some words toward Adam and proceeded to walk away. I now had an idea that Cristie was playing me dirty with her boss, but I had no concrete evidence. Why else would she be upset about me working directly across from her store unless she had something to hide? I couldn't see that far the way my eyesight was decreasing, but again I did not get this job to spy but to have more funds around the holiday season. Once the Halloween store closed, the same owners opened a Christmas store and asked if I wanted to be the assistant manager, and I was honored to accept this position.

One night I walked over to Cristie's store from *Yankee Candle* after cutting my finger when I was opening boxes of shipment and now required a first aid kit. There wasn't one in the store for whatever reason, so I walked into her store and proceeded to step toward the back. It was about 8:45 p.m.; I opened the back door and said, *"Babe, I need your first aid kit."* She walked out the bathroom door in an astute deceptive manner, as if someone was in there that my eyes shouldn't see. She was now acting frantic and put this Band-Aid on my finger in a manner that was not her character. I walked out of the store, made a left and waited for 20 seconds while looking directly at the store entrance. I walked back in, and she was busted! She said, *"He just walked in,"* and of course, my vocabulary was not proper as she was lying directly to my face! You can't un-honk a horn, and I could not forget the lie casted towards me. I walked back to my store and started getting ready to close, and Cristie sent me a text stating that her boss was going to give her a ride home! I'm slowly losing everything, and my temper was the first thing I lost for many reasons on many occasions, and she was no longer fanning my flames of happiness but dousing my fire with aggravation due to lack of loyalty! Did the fire in the furnace just dissipate?

CHAPTER 9

WHAT DO I DO NOW?

My friend J.Z. called me a week later and was in a panic, expressing to me that his girlfriend's younger sister was missing! J.Z. stated that he might know her whereabouts and asked if I could go scout with him. I picked him up, took him where he needed to go and was glad that I would be utilized to help another human in such a manner. I then received a phone call from Cristie, who wanted to hang out with me after she clocked out from work, but I was currently busy tending to a friend who needed assistance in a major way. Minimizing my feelings, she rancorously expressed to me, *"Forget you; enjoy your friends because this relationship is over!"* I short-circuited and felt like an ice cube being thrown into a beverage and internally cracked instantly! I was tending to an urgent matter and lost my relationship for helping a friend, and this was a very selfish act, and the breakup had nothing to do with my bitterness, and I didn't see that coming.

In this case, I did not have to check the oil with my attitude because this was all her, and Cristie needed a reason to leave and was waiting for an opportunity to execute. Every rose has its thorn, and I was hers! The love was long gone, and that was mostly my fault, and this was her way out! *What do I do now?* I had to redirect my energy elsewhere, so I bought the video game *"G.O.W. 1 & 2"* and drifted into an epic game of Greek gods and mythical creatures. I would wake up and play before work, come home after work to resume the game and play until I went to bed and kept repeating this cycle for six days. I beat both games in less than a week and buried my sadness in the process. I thought to myself that if I was going to be blind, I was going to take advantage of my eyesight before it was stripped from me! Did I mention I have abandonment issues? I'm pretty sure it's evident. Tick-Tock!

Jaclyn worked in the mall around this time, and I recall being in my car outside the front entrance when she approached me and questioned, *"What's up darling?"* I started explaining with a crackling voice how I won't be able to work or drive anymore because I was going to be 100% blind very soon. Her eyes began flooding with tears quite rapidly, and my heart broke because I saw hers break for mine; months later, the sight in my right eye was gone! One night I was working until 9:30 p.m. and was nervous to drive home. My vision was slipping away, and because I wasn't used to operating with one eye during evening hours, this became quite the conundrum. I left the mall and made a left turn on the main road but turned too quickly and started heading towards oncoming traffic on Route 6.

People were flashing me, so I knew I was on the wrong side of the road and had to cross over, but I reacted like a deer in headlights, not knowing what to do for a few seconds because my eyesight during this dark hour allowed me to assess many things in an obscured view. There was a building on the right side of the road that was barely visible, and somehow, I crossed over the pavement, over some meadows and managed to end up in the parking lot of this structure. I was nervous but unwilling to call anybody for help since it was late, and I was stubborn in certain areas. A state trooper pulled up behind me, and after he stepped out of his vehicle and approached me, he questioned if everything was okay! It was dark, and I couldn't tell the difference between the grass and concrete, and my headlights didn't help either since they weren't too bright. I replied, *"I'm ok, my blood sugar is dropping, and I just need to rest until I'm well."* I showed him my license and diabetic identification card, and he instructed me to have a great evening.

As I examined the image in my rear-view mirror, I was observing the police vehicle and knew I needed to follow that car to find my way out! I couldn't just take off since the vision of my surrounding was limited, so I took a deep breath and slowly began driving. I was clueless as to where I was until I saw a car pass me, and I said, *"Follow that car!"* I hit the gas petal, got off the grass and found solid ground, and since I was able to see the white line on the right side of the road, it was easy for me to get on the highway, stay in the right lane and follow taillights of another until I saw my exit. It took me over an hour for a twelve-minute drive to arrive home, and I didn't know what would happen, but I knew that I could no longer drive at nighttime! *What do I do now?*

The next morning, the District Manager walked into the store as the traffic volume was high with customers, and I instantly became apprehensive. Thirty minutes later she requested for me to come in the back with her and I was annoyed that Paulie knew that she was coming to visit and never informed me, his assistant! The DM informed me that I *"failed"* a secret shopper report with a ninety, and I stated the scores percentile is an A minus on an exam! She swiftly changed the course of the conversation and brought up my background check and stated that it came back, and I was relieved of my duties! In the moment I thought in my head, "It took a year for a background check to come back?" She thanked me as I handed her the store key and expressed to her that a little integrity would've been nice to see because I was not being fired for a "failed" score but rather because of the background check. I left the premises and proceeded home after inquiring the video game store if they needed any assistance, and after all that transpired, I grew exhausted and needed to remain tranquil because I am only one person and can only take so much!

This upcoming Monday morning, an altercation with my parents had occurred, and since there was tension in the atmosphere, I got into my car and fled. I was very disturbed, but of course, I would be distraught; I was going blind; plus, there is a spiritual battle happening in this world, and my parents were illuminating me with the light of God while I was lost in the shroud darkness of the world. I concluded that this evening I would try to reconcile things by purchasing a large sausage and pepperoni pizza with a box of canned iced tea for my family. The pizza shop was five minutes away from my house, and although I always buckle up, this time I chose not to do so and slid on black ice while making a sharp right turn to avoid colliding into another car as I was heading towards the hill of my residence. For lack of not speeding, my car was about to gain exhibition points and become airborne.

I never closed my eyes because I had to be aware of the direction the shards of glass were flying, so I grabbed my cross, which was dangling from my rear-view mirror, saw Cristie's face in a flash and the next I knew, I was standing on the inside of the roof to my Nissan. Silva was in his cousin Anthony's car, adjacent to where I flipped my Sentra, when he ran out of his cousin's vehicle while it was not completely stopped, injuring himself in a minor way just to make sure his best friend was okay! I escaped out of the driver's window without a scratch but had to be careful since shards of glass were scattered everywhere. I called my house and told my mother that I flipped my car and was down the street, and once that conversation ended, my brother and dad arrived in minutes to my location. I called Adam, who was in the mall parking lot, and he arrived at my setting in roughly five minutes, meaning the person he was riding along with was clocking in at over 100mph.

The Police and Fire Department arrived, and Silva's family came to my assistance, as their home was a jump, skip and hop away from the accident and provided me with a blanket to remain warm. When my father saw how attentive Adam and Silva's family were toward me, he was very impressed because neither party had ever met Dad, and he observed a clear connection between Adam, this family and myself. I questioned out loud, *"Where's my pizza?"* I didn't understand why one of the firefighters said he would take it back to the firehouse. My twenty-dollar pizza now had toppings of glass shards, so it wasn't going to be digested by anyone. A State Trooper asked me some questions, and I lied to him about wearing my seatbelt and briefly; after this, the Fire Marshall approached me and uttered that he knew I didn't have my seatbelt on because if I did, it would have snapped my neck in his opinion. The one time I decided not to put on my seatbelt, God allowed my life to be spared. I told myself that the enemy was trying to destroy me for attempting to make things right with my parents while God protected me and made it evident that my time was not to be completed at this hour. Talk about a spiritual battle in progress! Perception is reality!

A few weeks passed, and since I had full coverage on my car, I was reimbursed a large amount and was excited to get behind the wheel again. Ceccil informed me that his brother's father-in-law was selling a Mustang, so I tested the car and was so impressed with its power that I purchased it immediately and drove it home illegally, with Seth following me since there were no plates! After the process of getting the car registered and insured days later, I went across the street from the mall to the gas station and inquired if any positions needed to be filled. The representative stated that they were seeking an overnight manager, so I asked for an application and was ecstatic about it. What better job could I acquire during this period than an overnight position? I was excited to be hired as the Overnight Manager in February and would arrive to work before dusk for safety precautions, and if need be, I would relieve the person who was on shift to go home early if they desired to do so. This gas station lost its alcohol license, so I was grateful that I didn't have to deal with minors trying to be sly about alcohol purchasing. This *Sunoco* was the hangout spot for many and before my shift started, there was always a cluster of people outside who smoked weed and would enter the gas station to purchase cigarettes and rollup paper products, just socializing and listening to music from their cars in the parking lot.

They were customers, so I had no reason to kick them off the premises despite their actions, and since I was the boss, nobody got in trouble because they were on my turf. My job was not to focus on what transpired outside but rather on what occurred inside the store unless that matter dealt with gas pumps. My shift was required to replenish the inventory, and it generally started at one in the morning when business was dead. I started the cigarette counts, which was the most challenging part of the job because prior to the shift start, the count must be done, and as each pack was sold, I had to keep a tab so that when the morning shift started, there was an accurate number in inventory. I completed most of my tasks this evening but stopped when I noticed a black limousine pulling into the station, and as the gentleman walked in, I was beyond joyful to see that it was Mr. Klopper, the man who inspired me to do great things with my life!

We both exchanged smiles and hugged, and it felt so great to see the man that elevated me the most when I needed hope to aid me during high school! I briefly mentioned how I lost sight in my right eye and that it was only a matter of time before I lost sight in my left. I treated him to a cup of coffee which I hope was good, and Mr. Klopper stated that if I ever needed a reference, he would love to be on that list! I continued the rest of my shift with a joyful smile on my face because inspiration is contagious, and this man always delivered that greatly.

Around this season, my friend Sean who was currently residing in *Florida*, was in town, and it was great that while I was working, Sean was staying at my house, and by the time I came home from work, my room was vacant, and Sean was out doing his thing. Sean is a brother in Christ, and since Dad walks with the Lord, they have had great fellowship with each other. Sean is like a son to my parents, and it was great to see my father permit someone to sleep in our home. Six years prior to this year, I remember having dinner with Sean's parents, and his dad reprimanded me when he noticed a pack of Newport 100's in my back pocket. He grabbed them and stated in a scolding manner, *"What's this? How long have you been smoking?"* It was a brief interrogation, but it was done out of love, and I respected his action because it is a nasty habit, and Sean's parents only wanted the best for me.

As my birthday was coming close, my sight was decreasing more, and the first week of August, I became weak in the knees when Cinderella walked into *Sunoco*, as many were asking things like, *"Wow, Steve, that's your lady?"* I stated that she was my ex, but if I wanted her, I could have her right now! Cinderella always made me feel confident, and with that confidence brought many attractions! I had a cover for my Mustang, so as it was getting darker outside, Cinderella's kids and her friend passed out in her vehicle, and we proceeded toward mine. We were in the vacant parking lot of the mall, but since I knew the security guards, they didn't bother me. She was one of the last two smiles I received before losing sight, and I was going to enjoy the type of relationship Cinderella, and I had one more time with my sinful heart!

Stephanie and I got in contact with each other a month later, and she asked me if I would like to go to *Manhattan* with her and a few others, including her younger sister. I accepted her invitation since Steph was single, and it was nice knowing I would spend time with her again. Since I never gave her enough attention that she deserved,

I wanted to make things right before my chance was ripped away from me. I went to pick up Stephanie, her sister and their friend, and as I was driving to the train station, nobody felt safe with me navigating, so I let Stephanie drive. I spent hours with her and had a blast in *New York City*. One of her friends even drove down there to pick us up, and we were eventually dropped off at the train station to retrieve my car and proceed towards her home.

We were platonic towards each other, and I recall observing her beautiful eyes as she said, *"You're different! You've never shown me this much attention!"* I told her that I was very sorry for never showing her enough courtesy, but as the evening ended, I feared dying on my way home, like literally, this is it, I'm toast! Stephanie and I kissed passionately before I left, and I told her that I would notify her once I arrived home. Trying to drive home around a landscape of trees and narrow roads in *Putnam Valley* at eleven at night was not only a difficult task, but it was scary and very dangerous, but with prayer and patience, I was guided home safely, but this was not done on my own accord, and someone above definitely guided me!

The next two months were very problematic with my eyesight, and unless you're visually impaired, you could never understand the battle I walk. The *Sunoco* headquarters wanted to provide diesel fuel for customers, so we would have to shut down for a month or so to receive this upgrade, and on October 2nd, I went into work knowing I'd be working a thirteen-hour shift and grew exhausted by this upcoming hour. I began sweeping the floor, but all that was coursing through my mind was, *"Didn't I clean that section already?"* A lot of diminutive black dots were scattered on the ground, and when I looked up and realized my view didn't view any better, I asked my coworker if he could watch the register while I rested my head, and he complied; fifteen minutes later I lifted my dome off the table, and my sight was more than 95% gone! The entirety of my eyesight was scoped out through a few pin holes, but I was glad that this was the closing day because it, too, was my last day of working here as the overnight manager!

I began texting Silva to inform him of what had just occurred and then my coworker's girlfriend said, *"You're texting your friend? You're not blind, liar!"* Thank you needle mover for my glucose elevating. I know she didn't just call me a liar while stating the truth. Tick-Tock! Now, keep in mind that I used to sell cellphones at *RadioShack*, so this task posed no problem with or without sight. I scoffed and called the day supervisor and explained to her that I was now blind, and she stated that she would clock me out and to be careful! Silva's mother Katie drove him to my job, and when he walked in, I provided him with the keys to my car and he escorted me outside and drove me home!

CHAPTER 10

CHAOTIC CONUNDRUM

During the next few weeks, I had multiple eye appointments, met a young college girl named *"Harley,"* and even had a job interview at *EB Games*. I recall the doctor saying that I had close to about five hundred lasers shot into each eye, and only my left eye could be salvaged! I don't recall how I met Harley, but it was nice to *"see"* an unfamiliar face who accepted me! When I left *Yankee Candle*, I applied to be a manager at *EB Games* but didn't expect a call back since all management positions were filled. The manager at the game store was unaware of my disability, nor was I willing to inform her about it. It was gratifying that she was willing to hire me as the Assistant Manager and had no knowledge of my visual impairment.

I told her I couldn't see well because my eyes were dilated, and she said, *"Once my assistant leaves, I'll call you Steven!"* Later that evening, Silva introduced me to this awesome guy Armando, his girlfriend *"Amber"* who I already knew for eight years and her sister *"Jennifer."* I smoked a pipe with Jennifer and became relaxed in conversation with Armando. Silva didn't smoke marijuana, and although I had no sight, I was not focused on my lack of view because of the positive vibe that was streaming from Armando. We remained there for about fifteen more minutes before departing, and as Silva left the room and said bye, Armando said, *"Bro, don't leave your boy behind!"* We all chuckled about it because I was just standing there waiting for guidance. Silva remarked, *"Oh right, I forgot he's blind!"* Once arriving in front of my home, Silva pulled into the driveway and asked me if I needed help, but I stated that I would manage. I called him within minutes and said, *"I walked into my house!"* He was glad, but I interrupted him and said, *"You didn't hear me right. I walked into my house... like face first into the door,"* and he unveiled his mirth, which was contagious, and my smile increased. Once I was in the basement, I was walking towards my bathroom but didn't see the door halfway opened, and I strode face-first into the corner of the door and busted my head open. I was now seasoned with aggravation because I was worn out from beating myself up every day. The next morning my mother informed me that my surgeries would be within the following week. I thank Mom tremendously for seeking the time to scout what doctors and or specialists I needed to visit to get the proper surgeries in order.

I was excited about this news because I was tired of smashing my knees into things, walking face-first into the corners of open doors and growing aggravated for injuring myself because of my visual impairment. All I wanted to do was see a shooting star, read a book, watch wrestling again, or play a video game, and none of these options were available! Well, the shooting star would come in abundance when I smacked my face into corners, but this was not exactly the celestial stellar I was seeking to view. Unfortunately, the time frame for the surgeries absolutely sucked because I was supposed to be Sean's best man at his wedding and would not be able to make it!

During this time, Mom took a lot of time off from work to bring me to my new eye specialist, who was referred to me by a different specialist. Managing my diabetes was more of a difficult task because I had to check my blood sugar and could barely see the screen on my glucometer. Taking my insulin wasn't an issue because I use a flex pen, so I had no need to withdraw insulin from a vial. As the day of surgery was approaching, I was not nervous and just wanted to be able to see again! What took me by surprise was having the numbing drop placed in my eye, followed by the doctor saying, *"Look straight and don't move,"* as he was inserting a needle directly into my eye. Feeling the needle tip penetrate the surface of my eye was dull but nerve-wracking. The surgery was a success; I looked like a cyborg as I had one blue eye and one brown. I had twenty-two stitches sown into my left eye, and attached was a donor's retina; a lot of steps needed to be done until my sight could be *"normal"* again.

Lee was doing his military thing, so I couldn't get in contact with him directly, but I did stumble across his dad's social media by accident and asked him if it was possible to deliver a message to his son. At first, I thought it was my friend Lee, but it turns out that they have the same name, so it was an honest mishap that worked in my favor. A few days later, Lee called me, and I was explaining how I lost my ability to see and how miserable I started to become since I was always independent and now had to rely on others. It was expressed to me that if my absence didn't affect *"them,"* my presence never mattered, so those who were around me were the ones that cared! As I was slowly pacing back and forth in my room, Lee said, *"Dude, I'll be there in two days!"* I acknowledged his words and went to go hang out with Danielle. Throughout this time, I noticed how my senses were expanding greatly, and since I was classified as blind, I was obligated to *"see"* an individual by listening to their tone. Listening to how people spoke was key because I could detect the difference in a person's character based on their pitch tone when one would exchange words with me, and this enabled me to hear the variance between people being truthful or suspicious, which was easy at times. I was *"Dare Devil"* in the sense that I heard more than my eyes could ever capture!

During the next couple of days, I felt drowned in annoyance because I was powerless to just get up and drive off in my car as I pleased. Danielle came over to pick me up, we went to Silva's residence, and a few of us were hanging out, and I was comfortable because I was with those who I knew would not allow anything bad to happen to me. Everybody was having fun and joking around when suddenly Silva dropped my sweatpants and took a Taser to my jewels. It was funny because everybody at the gas station now saw me standing in my yellow boxers, but it didn't matter much because I couldn't even observe anybody observing me. Silva, Danielle, and others started laughing harder, and my response while giggling was, *"Silva, when I find you, wherever you are, I'm going to punch you!"* He chuckled and replied, *"You have to find me first!"* I began laughing more while holding my sweatpants up because I didn't know if he would repeat this stunt again. I was glad the taser batteries were low in power and let me just add that this was an electrifying experience. I received a phone call and heard, *"Hey, I'm around, where are you?"* I mentioned to this individual my whereabouts, and within ten minutes, the same voice said, *"Steve, I told you I'd be here!"* Lee delivered his promise of coming to my assistance when I needed additional help. My parents work in *New York City*, my sister was busy as a schoolteacher, and my brother was employed out of state, so who could I rely on to help me with my dilemma? Once the gathering concluded, Silva drove Lee and me back to my parents' house.

At first, Dad was reluctant to let anybody that he did not know to stay in his house, let alone spend countless nights there with nobody else present! Once he observed the personality of Lee and the genuine respect we had, the image altered itself. I explained my friendship with Lee, and my mother was happy that I had another friend willing to assist further. Lee was the person who fashioned three meals a day for me and attended every doctor's appointment, and all I did with my spare time was listen to my iPod when I wasn't with my friends because that's all I could do! Lee came to my rescue, although it was, he who needed rescuing, yet he had no idea until he stepped foot into the church I attend!

My parents grew to love him as another son, and it was nice to have the extra company, but sometimes there were scenarios where Lee performed foolishly. For example, Lee and I decided to visit *"E,"* and when we arrived, Lee almost reversed my car off a ledge while trying to parallel park my Mustang. Not exactly the best kickoff from a long return, and the back end of my vehicle was approximately five feet off the ground, and we were just dangling there while people in that area looked dumbfounded at how Lee put us in such a predicament. I became rancorous since this was my vehicle, and it was just a matter of time before it was going to topple over, so *"E"* said that he would try to assist. Twenty minutes passed, and a gentleman with a white truck reversed into this small complex, allowing my rear wheels to grip his flatbed so *"E"* could drive forward. Once this was over, my blood pressure went back to normal, but my blood sugar was elevated.

Later this week, Harley called and asked if Silva could drive me to her college dorm to hang out. Silva wasn't busy, so he was enthusiastic to drive my Mustang, so Lee tagged along, and we made our commute. We were there for a few hours and had a lot of fun telling stories and laughing with Harley's roommates. Lee was trying to show off how he could perform multiple handstands differently, and everybody observing had a kick out of it because he did it while lifting his body, spun on his head, and was even dared to do it nude. I vocalized to Harley and the others that I was grateful to be blind because this was an image I was not trying to view. During our travel home, Silva couldn't stop talking about how I locked myself in the bathroom dorm, which was definitely a good laugh for our inside joke. The following week Harley asked if Silva, Lee, and I wanted to attend a Pre-Halloween party on the college grounds. We came to a consensus to go, and I was excited to attend another road trip with my buddies. Harley appeared to have a crush on me, and if she was willing to accept my flaws as she saw them, then it was evident that I would do the same. She introduced me to her male college friends and explained to them that I was blind and to be careful around me.

I've never been to a college party, and to hear all the chaotic shenanigans around, I needed to rely on Silva for everything! He was my eyes, navigator, and chauffeur and literally looked out for me at all costs! The campus security started to inform everybody that the partying was over, so we three stooges vacated the premises and proceeded back home, and through everything I was encountering, the reason for me not being oppressed in depression was having my music and observing the loyalty of others towards me!

On Halloween evening, Silva, Lee, and I went for a joyride and were contemplating where we would go and what we would be doing, so these two decided to enter a local bar because it was themed Halloween. Silva asked if I wanted to come inside, but I refused and stayed in my car, blaring my music. Although I couldn't see much, that didn't mean I couldn't see. They were inside approximately fifteen minutes before returning to my vehicle, and Lee obtained a woman's number! It was expressed to me that Claudia was beyond attractive, and although I did not believe them, once I viewed her, she looked like a Columbian Wonder Woman, and I was speechless! We, the men, decided to go pick up Harley from her home and then to Silva's house for a "beer & bonfire" evening. By the conclusion of this evening, I was dating Harley and cherished her for not judging me for an ailment I did not ask to acquire. I knew that Lee had limited time to spend with me, but he decided to go AWOL (Absent With Out Leave) and extended his stay so I had care and was not solo. He expressed that he never leaves a fallen soldier behind, and I, in return, was grateful to hear that articulated!

The following day he and an old friend, *"James,"* brought me to my eye specialist for a process that consisted of my left eye being sown shut with twelve stitches. The doctor said that this needed to be done because my eye was too dry, and the drops required had to stay flowing on and around my eyeball. She often appeared distraught, and my buddies witnessed her speech toward me, and she would even elevate her voice, so everybody heard her, and it came off as if she was shouting because she was indeed yelling. I was upset that she was the only one on these grounds to do this procedure, so I had no alternative options. This was physically and mentally painful because I was incapable of seeing again, and without a cane, I prepared to walk into many things again! A few days later, Lee made breakfast for me, and when he reentered my room to present this meal, he noticed I was in a pool of my own sweat, incoherent and knocked out on my bed!

Lee or Desiree called 9-1-1, and I recall nothing of the issue because I was in a diabetic shock. Once I arrived at the emergency room, Desiree indirectly made me very upset, saying that I needed help because I was *"crazy"!* Seriously? I just lost my ability to see over a month ago, my left eye was sown shut, and now when I have this diabetic episode where I'm incoherent, I'm crazy? When the blood sugar drops extremely low, this commonly causes brain fuel deprivation, resulting in brain failure. This can also allow the individual to have a seizure or go into a coma. The best way to explain a hypoglycemic attack like this is, *"The camera (my eye) is on, but there is no videotape to record anything."* Once I recovered as a result of the glucose provided, I still had no knowledge of what had just happened.

Desiree and I are cut from the same cloth yet complete opposites, even at the age of twenty-four, and she will never understand any of the side effects of a high or low blood sugar. My father observed all that I was encountering and expressed to me that he had me in his cell phone contact as *"Braveheart!"* It meant a lot since Dad and I weren't close, but what he did see was the struggle of his son fighting for strength yet again, and although I had lack of sight, I could see my dad as a sober man, and he was abstemious for seven years now, and he wasn't a seething person anymore. Just like anything in life, time changes everything, and our relationship as father and son grew to be better as time progressed! Wow, I didn't see the coming.

Danielle and I were communicating on the phone early this afternoon when she told me that her car was hardly operable after I asked if she could pick me up to hang out. As Danielle is my best friend, I told her that she could transport herself using my Mustang, and she was ecstatic about this privilege. As the holiday approached, Harley, Lee and I were with Danielle and James for Thanksgiving, and I appreciated my friendship with them. Unfortunately, sometime after this day, James became a wolf in sheep's clothing because of an alarming situation that turned him into exactly that. He tried to save money by working on his truck, and it ended up collapsing on his chest, and in time, he was lifeless! When he was revived, his former self was no longer in existence, and everybody, including his wife, took notice.

James had volunteered to be my chauffeur, so my mom could return to work since she used all her personal days for my appointments. That proposal came at a cost and was a price I would never want to pay. James always had a thing for the females I dated in high school and was more upset that the ones who dated me never liked him, but almost ten years later, he completed his mission after Lee went back to do his Navy service. It's foul what James did behind my back, knowing I could literally do nothing about it, but nonetheless, I called Harley and asked where she was, and she told me that she was at James' place. There was no pity in her voice for me, and I was wounded deeply because he only aided me to get close to her, and I sat in my room a shattered mess and prayed for healing! James made it very simple to cut the tie by handing me the scissors, and I was obliged since I had no choice. On another note, later this week, the pressure in my eye increased to the number sixty-eight, and I was informed that my eye could implode at this level! Tick-Tock!

I was crying continuously and just wanted to faint, and Desiree stopped everything she was doing to drive me to *Manhattan* to get this resolved, and I couldn't express how thankful I was for her to be present. I took three Tylenol PMs and passed out, only to wake up two and a half hours later with a chronic migraine and temples throbbing, like I needed this right now! The physician was able to place drops in my eye to lower the constriction, and sometime later, it was back to normal!

When Lee was still present, he realized that his visit to *New York* was not about me but about the comfort that God would provide him through faith. Unless one knows what salvation means through Jesus Christ, it's easily rejected, and Lee now understood the meaning! God would use a broken person like me to help save Lee, which proves that God will use any person's circumstance in any condition to see them be saved and turn to faith because, as Hebrews 11:6 says, <u>"Without faith, it is impossible to please God."</u> Anyway, moving forward, I frequently relished the words of encouragement articulated by Danielle as she told me, *"Don't sweat, Harley, because someone loyal is out there waiting for you!"* We decided to go to *Philadelphia* to visit a friend of hers after a massive blizzard swept the land, and before this trip was in effect, we chose to go sledding with Silva's brother Vinnie and sister Nicole.

When we arrived on the field, Danielle realized that we needed some extra gear, so she and Nicole left briefly, and I walked and talked with Vinnie. He told me to climb up a fence and jump over to the baseball field since that was our destination, but on its way was another *chaotic conundrum* waiting to unravel itself. There was about a foot and a half of snow, so I wasn't worried about my landing, but I was hesitant to jump because Vinnie had a boulder size snowball that could generate a loud thud upon impact. He said, *"I won't throw it!"* I kept faking my leap off the fence while keeping my grip on the pole because he pretended multiple times to launch this snow boulder.

I finally said to myself that if I do a one hundred eighty-degree turn, it'll hit my back, and I'll be okay! I sprang off, crouched, and turned in midair like I was going to perform a cannonball. I braced myself for the impact of this boulder-like snowball, and the thud projected loud since it hit my backside before my feet hit the snow. I couldn't tell how much space I had between where I was and where I was landing since I was now legally blind and saw nothing but white on white. When I landed, my right knee connected to my chin, and I gave myself the wrestling move known as *"G.T.S.,"* which stands for *"Go to sleep."* Laying on my back in ten-degree weather, I started sweating and began removing articles of clothing one by one, and as Vinnie wanted to assist me, I instructed him to let me be because if I were to be helped up, I would have collapsed right back down from being so weak in the knees. The energy of defeat was within me!

Once I got myself collected, it was time to go down this slope, and once Danielle returned with Nicole, this activity would be ready to unveil its wonders as this was my first time doing such an activity. Danielle pushed the sled, and I was excited yet nervous because as I was gaining speed, another raft with two girls collided into me, and I heard Danielle asking from afar, *"Oh no, are you ok?"* Once the sled came to a halt, I got off and picked it up, turned around, and another sled flew into my legs immediately, knocking me face-first into the ground like a snow angel. I heard Danielle, Vinnie and

Nicole laughing hard, and during my time on the ground, I was laughing too, saying to myself, *"How does a blind guy get hit twice within a minute apart?"* I didn't see that coming, and this fortuitous event was not only comical, but after that encounter, my sledding days were now over! The hardest task for me was trusting others for things I was used to doing on my own, and Adam, Danielle and Silva were the main people I associated with after Lee departed, so I wasn't alone.

Celebrating Thanksgiving with Danielle was amazing because I enjoyed her cooking and even slumbered over her house during Christmas with Adam, and it was nice to not be deserted for the holidays after being dumped without notice. I was blessed with those who understood me, and during my weakness, they wanted to bring the best out of me! I often thanked them and realized that they simply encouraged what was already inside of me to rise! If these three were not around, my life would be significantly different, and I'm not saying I couldn't make it in life without them, but I'm glad I don't have to, and they greatly looked out for me!

CHAPTER 11
ROCK BOTTOM TO WILLPOWER

I dreaded the wintertime for many reasons, and during midwinter, I ended up in the emergency room due to health concerns and was admitted. I was seasoned with misery because nobody was there, my eye was sown shut, and I wanted Max! Suddenly I heard a voice say, *"Yo, Steve, your favorite artist is in town!"* I questioned, *"Dru?"* as I heard his voice. He said, *"Yeah, kid, I'm here, bro! Silva told me you were in the hospital, and I've come to comfort you with a story from the book of Job."* It's pronounced as "Jobe." This is one of the sixty-six books that create the Bible and I have never read this book before, and as Andrew was reading to me, it was revealed that Job lost a lot, such as his animals from thieves, a fire burned his property and even killed all of his servants. In addition, the house of Job's son was knocked down by a storm that killed all of Job's children.

Job was the most righteous in all the *East* according to God, but even Job complained and blamed God as the mayhem took place and by the end of this book, Job humbled himself, and God blessed him with everything he lost tenfold! Andrew expressed to me that it didn't matter that I lost my sight because if I humble myself and not focus on the situation, but rather trust God with my situation, He can turn it around and bless me abundantly! This visit from Andrew meant a lot, and he knew this story would aid me to prosper! That is why he is my favorite and only barber because he always has my best interest.

Spring arrived, and over the course of winter, with three months of healing, the sight in my left eye was no longer what it was after my procedure took place, and I grew with optimism and could see clearer as time advanced. Scattered pieces of my former lifestyle wanted to be assembled again because I was still not finished being who I wanted to be as opposed to becoming a man of faith. Danielle's vehicle was reinstated to its full potential, and since she no longer needed mine, once she returned it, I drove to see Adam and a mutual friend *"Casper"* who had his own place; and let me just say it was very rewarding to have the ability to drive again! Upon arriving, I saw this adorable female having a great time socializing, is shorter than me, well figured and happened to smoke weed. I didn't recognize Jennifer until she asked me about my sight. She saw that I was walking and driving during daylight hours, not needing the help of anyone like I did when I met her with Silva. After we spoke, Jennifer told me that she wanted to date me and wasn't going to wait forever, so we made it official. If she had a warning label like prescription drugs, I would've seen the side effects, but nothing was visible until she was sober minded!

During the very first week of dating Jennifer, I got her pregnant! My mother didn't know that Jenn was antenatal but told me that I had a choice, leave the relationship or leave the house! Call it mother intuition, if you will, but my mom was not wrong about why I should have left Jenn, yet she had no understanding of why I couldn't abandon this relationship. I wasn't dubious about my response, and it was unquestionable to move out with Jennifer and her family because this was not the ultimatum to present to me under the new-found discovery, which was not currently shared with others. Jennifer was relocating anyway, so it was nice to start fresh! On the second day of living with her, it was around five a.m., and I stated, *"If you can't wake me up later, take that soda, lift my head, and make sure I drink it!"* About four hours later, I was in a pool of sweat, unconscious and suffering from another hypoglycemic attack.

She panicked, forgot what I had explained hours prior, and thought I was faking. Her sister Amber walked in the room and told Jennifer to call 9-1-1 and to stop assaulting me because Jenn was apparently punching me in my face, according to her sister, and was even hitting me in my jewels, but seriously, any person in their right mind would know that this was not a bogus act. She could've punched me into a coma, but I'm just grateful I was unconscious not to feel her strike because I probably would have thrown her out the window; being as I was in an incoherent state! Don't worry, we were on the ground floor; in the worst-case scenario she still would've been fine.

When I was escorted to the ambulance with Jennifer, this kleptomaniac Amber stole my two-hundred-dollar iPod from my room. Years of collecting my music and pictures just vanished in mere seconds because of her addiction. Amber stole my personal belongings to buy drugs and even took my spare diabetic syringes to obtain the high while I was in the emergency room recovering after a near-death experience. Tick-Tock! I was fueled with rage, the damage was done, and I couldn't reverse anything that happened. I was living in a house where sin played a serious role on a daily basis, and just because I went to church didn't make me any more of a better person than anybody here who didn't attend a church service. Armando and I got along well, but we didn't hang out because we loathed each other's girlfriends.

Jon and Jaclyn were living down the road from us, and it was thrilling to have my friend of eight years and his wife, who has my utmost respect, in walking distance. I was the guy that people enjoyed hanging around, but it never dawned to think on *"why"* until the patterns started to repeat themselves. Adam was within walking distance and commuted on foot from his place to my location to hang out. We decided that we were going to make this a semi *"blast from the past"* and hang out with *"E"* like the good old times. I permitted Adam to drive the Mustang, and because he is one of my best friends, it was humbling to see him with such joy for having this opportunity. The only difference this time was that my girlfriend was my shadow, and wherever I went, she followed.

The four of us had a few hours of fun, and I was ready to call it a night. Adam drove *"E"* to his house to conclude the evening, and it was expressed by *"E"* that he wanted to continue hanging out because the night was still young. It wasn't even nine o'clock, and my intuition said not to do it, but because I apparently live to please others, I granted his wish, and the night sustained itself, and the ruse rolled out from here. Time rushed exponentially, and before midnight would strike, Adam reminded me that he needed to be home soon, and since he couldn't drive *"E"* home, I allowed *"E"* to spend the night, and Adam would return in the morning with my car.

At around ten a.m., I walked outside to see a few people gathered by my Mustang, and it was notable that Jenn was uncharacteristically silent. *"E"* stated that he left his cigarettes inside the house, and Jenn shadowed him, and that's when a red flag fashioned itself since she is normally my shadow. I felt that negative energy ready to ignite out of me, but I needed proof before combusting with rage! As they both walked back to the group, I followed them with my eyes and, in minutes, requested for Jennifer to follow me inside the home, and once we entered our bedroom, she dreadfully enunciated to me that she had sex with *"E"* on the floor of our bedroom, after giving me a Tylenol PM! Seriously?

He repudiated everything and became rapidly defensive. I heard the guilt in his tone, cursed him out and told him to kick rocks! *"E"* knew he did wrong, and substance abuse of any kind can take control over someone if their illness gets to that level, but even with that said, there is no excuse for the actions committed! Jennifer pleaded her sorry, and I foolishly forgave her, even though this was a reprehensible act. She was the drug that I needed to discard, and I wasn't seeking an antidote, and the solution was to simply relinquish this affiliation with her. Foolishly I felt that I could still help her become an improved individual! The majority of my disability money would be exchanged for a temporary sedative that didn't fix her issue; it just concealed her hostility very well. I would purchase ounces of marijuana for her pleasure, so she was not rancorous. I discovered that I was dating a bipolar female who did not believe in taking prescribed medication to service her disorder. This would be very detrimental and a trigger to my physical health with my diabetes and emotional well-being, which produced mental anguish and made me spiritually dead. She would wake up angry, and my goal was to tame that fire within her, and as we were growing closer, it made sense to invite her to church, especially since she was an angry pregnant mess! I was living in sin and knew I needed to transform many of my immoral ways because I was living for myself and not for God!

I allowed Jennifer's expectations to disrupt my character, and we were the couple that went to church like many and the minute we left, we were aggressive pot smokers who cussed and had sex daily. I'm not a sinner because I sin, I sin because I am a sinner, and it's built into everybody's DNA, whether people choose to believe it or not, but it doesn't mean it's okay for me to practice my sin. I can't be sinless, but I can practice my sin less!

Two months later, Jennifer told me that she had a doctor's appointment, so her dad drove us to the clinic so she could be evaluated. After she signed in, we waited about fifteen minutes before I went outdoors and was thrilled to know how my child's progress was doing in Jennifer's small frame of a body. As she was being called in, she said that she would return soon, so I decided to remain outdoors. After a half hour, I began to grow anxious, and when she finally waltzed outside, she was drowning in tears and said, *"I lost our baby!"* She then told me that she had an abortion, broke down in my arms, dropped to her knees and sobbed with her face looking downward! My face darkened with disappointment, but I know that God's forgiveness, when confessed in truth and repentance, is important because, to my belief, understanding and perception, this is murder despite those who may disagree with it! Once the baby has a heartbeat, it's a living being and my kid was not lost, they were taken!

Jennifer robbed me of what I've waited for since I was younger, and whenever people questioned what I wanted to be when I grew up, I always replied that no matter the occupation, I'll dominate it, but as far as what to be; well, that's a dad! I wanted to raise my kid better than I was, and I wanted to feel that parental love that only a parent could feel when they see their child for the first time, and I was stripped of this opportunity. My child never had the ability to live on earth, but he or she is in a realm where sin does not reside, nor are there tears, pain or suffering of any kind. I thought to myself that my child is in heaven, and I will definitely be excited when our first encounter occurs in His kingdom one day, but to even have that be a possibility, I need to know Who the Creator of heaven is and what He did to save humanity and I found the answer in the bible! Not long after this unfortunate event with Jennifer, my mother texted me and said that my fat boy Max wasn't doing well and would be put down. My family came to pick me up with Jennifer, and my four-legged son had his shirt on him that says, *"I still live at home with my parents,"* and boy, was he excited to see me again, wagging his nugget tail. He ate his final meal at the animal hospital, and within minutes Desiree said, "I think he's still breathing" and the nurse said, "No he's gone!" Max died in my arms, and my toughest battle at this point was physically letting go of him! I plummeted to my knees before exiting, and my eyes flooded more than any previous time I have ever cried and couldn't believe my little boy was gone! This was my biggest breakup, and it tore me apart because I wasn't ready to let go! I even recall my dad saying in the vestibule, *"Wow... I want a cigarette."* The loss of Max was devastating to all of us! I was dropped off where I was picked up and got high to numb the pain. I was down for countless nights, so for countless nights, I was high and wept the sobs for weeks!

One year later, Jennifer and I relocated to another location five minutes from where we were living prior, and this time around, Armando and Amber did not live with us. My mother picked me up one afternoon and brought me to an eye appointment where I needed the surface of my eye to be scrapped because I had a calcium deposit building a thick layer on the surface of my eye as a result of the milky drops I was still taking when I had my eye sown shut, and it caused my sight to be distorted. It turned out that while this procedure was being done, Jon was with Jennifer getting high. My mother transported me back to where I lived only to get me about thirty minutes later because it was expressed by the office who contacted my mom that my eye could possibly develop an ulcer if I didn't return to the office. My mother was a great support beam and drove over two hours in distance to make sure I was in better condition. Jon would capitalize on his desire to mate with my girlfriend and cheat on his wife during my absence! Tick-Tock!

Jennifer told me the following day, and I called him, left a voice mail, and threatened him! I stated that I would inform Jaclyn, so he had better get his behind to my location. The countdown was in motion, and when he arrived in approximately ten minutes, I told Jon to have integrity and hurt me with the truth and not comfort me with a lie, but he denied the whole thing. Jennifer shouted, *"Jon, why are you lying?"* This kerfuffle between them made me feel like a volcano, ready to erupt with all this pressure developing within, and I told him that I was going to assault him and communicate this information to his wife! I also told him that when someone is in a hole, they need to know when to stop digging because they will eventually bury themselves. It turned out that this wasn't the first time this activity had taken place between them, and once this was exposed to me, I informed Jaclyn immediately! The thing about me is that I am a nice guy until I am not, and at this point, I was a ticking time bomb. I knew that Satan would hit me with everything that could break me since I was dating a nonbeliever, hanging out with unbelievers, and living with bad company! Over the course of time, people were taking my kindness for weakness, and I was very foolish to allow it! I remember attending church and hearing Matthew 6:14-15 which says, *"For if you forgive others for their transgressions, (wrongdoings) your heavenly Father will also forgive you. But your Father will not forgive your transgressions if you do not forgive others."* There were many times when I didn't want to follow this scripture, but this was not stated as an option; it is presented as a statement!

    Thinking about the sins of my past years allowed me to observe my present wrongdoings, and because I wanted forgiveness for the bad deeds of my historic ways, I had to forgive ungracious *"E,"* fickle Jon, and the recalcitrant Jennifer! The power of forgiveness provided a path of freedom for me instead of allowing my frustration to keep me bound to these chains. A wise leader will make peace with their past! If I didn't escape this rock bottom, it would cost me or be my demise! I was keen to become what God wanted me to be but failed to understand that I couldn't be effective if I am living in these sinful conditions. I was trying to elevate confidence in Jennifer while Satan was using her to descend me to her level, and he had a *"home advantage"* since not one person in this abode was a follower of Jesus, so darkness was always present! I couldn't just pick and choose when I wanted to serve Him; I had to be consistent, stop pleasing people, discover who I am and live for Him! Jon sealed his fate when he chose my girlfriend and weed over his marriage and child! Jon and Jaclyn parted ways, and I was still illogically with Jennifer, and I'll blame it on the dopamine synced with idiocy, so now the trail I was seeking was from the point of *rock bottom to willpower*! I heard a voice that told me I still had one task to complete and to shield myself!

The relationship was hanging on its final thread, and the task of sharing the good news of the gospel with her was still His mission. She and I were attending church on a normal basis, and on this one Sunday evening, I questioned Jennifer if we could watch a Christian movie. We settled in, and by its conclusion, she said, *"I got it! I understand why this is important!"* I felt accomplished because this was all I struggled to hear from her for over two years of this teetered relationship. I decided to get a beverage, but before going downstairs, I told Jennifer to ask God for forgiveness for all her wronging. When I returned to the room, I asked her if all was well, and she nodded yes with a poise attribute and then began playing garbage rap music. I asked Jenn if she could get me a Tylenol PM so I could rest, and as she left the room, I prayed for God to deliver me the sign on which I leave the premises because I heard a voice tell me that I was to no longer be here! She handed me this pill, and I was out like a light within the hour.

The next morning Jennifer attempted to wake me, pushing my right shoulder as I was facing the wall saying, *"Babe? Babe?"* Here's a quick fact about me, if nobody is getting hurt, the house is not on fire, and you're not checking my sugar level or providing me insulin, leave me alone and let me rest because when I'm disturbed from a deep sleep, I might wake up exasperated and that's not fair to me! I finally turned over and yelled, *"What?"* Now before I explain what was said to me, keep in mind that I have been knocked out for over twelve hours and, as a person with diabetes, should not go this long without having my sugar checked. As a result, my glucose was over six hundred and as known, people with diabetes with high glucose levels can become short-tempered because of an imbalance within the body, but it doesn't end here because she did not give me a Tylenol PM; she provided me 25mg of her Seroquel. This is known as an anti-psychotic to treat certain mental mood conditions such as schizophrenia and or bipolar.

So not only did I have a chemical imbalance on top of an elevated blood sugar while being disturbed from my sleep, but she stated in a miserable manner, *"I just wanted to tell you that in two and a half years of dating, I cheated on you thirteen times and with two of your best friends on more than one occasion."* That voice that said, *"Shield Yourself,"* was now understood! I needed Heaven to rescue me because I'm about to fall apart or be very ticked off. Time was suddenly motionless, and a darkness that I never knew could exist on such a scale was awoken within me, and I felt like hell was about to break loose! **TICK-TOCK BOOM!** This news was so nauseating that if my stomach were hurting, this would've been the jump start to my vomiting! I jumped out of the bed, chased her down the stairs, and she bolted out the front door. I wasn't going to make a scene outside, so Jenn had no idea of my location when she came back in the house. As she approached the living room, I walked out of the bathroom, shut the front door and was terrified for her because I didn't know how I was going to react once I knew she couldn't run anywhere.

Either I was going to be in control, or I was going to allow God to take the wheel! I noted her with the house phone in hand and questioned, *"Who are you calling?"* Petrified and trembling, she replied, *"Nobody,"* and hung up the phone. Knowing that for every action, there is an equal reaction, she should have confessed it to God and let it be, but Jennifer always looks for conflict, and now she found one with me! We had an intense five-minute fight and when her hands went up, I smacked her left hand which went towards her face and Jennifer's eye started becoming black and blue. That wasn't my intention, but that's the unfortunate situation that unfolded! Jenn walked over towards me and brashly stated, *"I have integrity!*

I could've hidden this from you, but at least I'm honest!" I told her that she couldn't even spell the word *"integrity,"* let alone try to convince me that she has what she does not possess! I expressed to her with heavy disgust that she was a lazy ass with a smart mouth, and I was aware that I needed to be on the winning team because no demon on earth or in hell is stronger than a will aligned with the Word of God, and He was my focus.

If I'm not with Him, I am against Him, so I summed it up into conclusion that she was the problem and not the solution! Jenn brought out the worst in people, including herself, and if she couldn't love the person in the mirror, how did I ever expect her to love me? I told her that this relationship was over and that I would arrange a ride back to my parent's home! The situation defused quickly, and I went to the bedroom, took a seat on the bed, closed my eyes, opened my mind, and knew that even through this madness, there was peace in my heart. This breakup was not temporary either! I was cashing out and wanted to part ways permanently, and Jennifer knew this was done, yet still tried to ingratiate me with lewd remarks but denied her!

This was how she kept her tentacles wrapped around me! Ironically, I recall Joe from church quoting Proverbs 7:27 that says, *"Her house is the way to Sheol, descending to the chambers of death,"* and I, for one, was not willing to follow that trail! The more I acknowledged myself in the flesh, the more I saw the flesh manifest, but I knew God didn't want that for me, and I told her that I would no longer fall prey to her deceptions, and it was evident that God wanted to separate this key from that lock, and I found this easy to accept and was done practicing this sin. Not everything that I faced could be changed, but I really couldn't change anything until it was faced, and after this ordeal, I threw in the towel and called it quits, and God became my spatula in the sense that He flipped me to see things from an improved perspective!

Jenn called me at 1:13 a.m. a week later, saying, *"I found your gold chain and cross, and I'm going to pawn it!"* I wasn't going to let that happen, and her new boyfriend was at her house, and he was her gateway to her newest substance of choice. She informed me that she wanted to buy cocaine, and I replied, *"You're not selling my cross or my chain!"* She remarked, *"You don't drive, you're blind, and you can't get here!"* I verbalized to her with an intense expression to say it again, and she repeated herself, thinking she was a boss and thought it was cute. I said, *"Ok, I'll see you soon!"* Jennifer retorted, *"What do you mean?"* I told her, *"I'll see you soon,"* and hung up the phone and got dressed.

I grabbed three bottles of water, used my flashlight on my phone and started my commute at 1:30 a.m., and keep in mind that it was not only dark, but I had no cane to guide me, and I was now on my way to walk a round trip of approximately twenty-three miles. When I'm determined and motivated, nothing will stop my persistence, and this walk was no picnic, and for a twenty-two-minute ride, it took me eleven-plus hours to do the majority of it on foot. While I was on my venture, Jennifer kept calling me, pleading for me to turn around, but I told her that this was no longer an option because she crossed that boundary line plenty of times and I won't lay down my arm, so she could get high from selling my property! I was on *Route Six* at four in the morning, which is a straight away, and my battery life on my cellphone dropped to ten percent, and sunrise was going to hit its peak in about an hour, so I had no need for concern since the darkness was ready to fade out.

Jennifer called me and said she would walk to meet me wherever I was, and my phone died once she addressed this. I had to be a couple of miles away from her home, and in about twenty minutes, I saw her from afar, and she was adjacent to me. Out of breath and out of water, I dropped to a knee and said, *"Steve, you did it!"* She crossed the street and was astonished that I had walked all this way for my belongings. I told her that the cross symbolizes my faith, and I won't allow her to pawn what is not hers. Pawning stolen property can result as a second-degree felony. I was a bit irritable because my legs were sore, and I was only at the 50% mark of this journey with no money, yet synchronously received joy for retrieving my property which she handed over. Jennifer instantly grew infuriated, and her persona altered like *"Jekyll and Hyde."* All I could vividly see was a miserable person attempting to spread desolation like a plague to all!

As I started my walk back home, her bipolar status remained active, and in an acrimonious manner, she began making fun of me for how short I am and yelled out loud, *"Nobody will ever want to be with a short blind loser like you!"* I was tired of being unethical, but she knew which buttons to push, and I just wish I knew where to find the "mute" button for her, but nonetheless, I turned around, and the chase began. I couldn't believe I started shuffling myself in the wrong direction of my home so that she could gain distance in her sprint from me. All she had to do was keep quiet and walk away, but she's content with being belligerent and waging conflict, and I disarmed her ability to wage it by walking away because there is no changing a person unless they want to seek support. <u>*"Bad company corrupts good morals,"*</u> and I was done being a product of her environment!

Jennifer continued her walk home, and within minutes a police car from her city crept behind me to ask questions. I informed the officer that I had walked about twelve miles so far and am legally blind, and the only means of my travel was to obtain my property, and now I'm going home! He asked, *"She's not going to say that that's hers, is she?"* My cross and chain were around my neck, and I remarked that if Jenn did, there was going to be a problem because I was done with her! He then questioned if I was threatening Jennifer, and I replied that he knew her family's background and that they weren't exactly righteous people. He agreed and said that he just needed to file the report since someone called 9-1-1, informing them of the altercation between the both of us. Once this was completed, I continued my journey back home and prayed that someone would assist me because my phone was dead, and my legs were tender.

Roughly two hours later, I was on the top of *Stony Street* and said to myself that it took me ninety minutes to walk up this hill, so going down shouldn't be too difficult of a task. All I wanted to do was go to bed, but with all this exercise, not only was I exhausted, but my blood-sugar started dropping, and I began to feel faint. I was on the left side of the road on a knee when a vehicle stopped about ten feet ahead of me, and this elderly gentleman questioned, *"You ok, son? Come here!"* I explained my situation, and he vocalized, *"Hey, listen, make me a promise, ok?"* I replied, *"Sure!"* He said, *"The next time you see someone needing help, promise me you'll help them by paying it forward!"* I made that promise to him, and he addressed for me to hop in the car. I thanked God for not forsaking me during this walk by the blessing of this man and for delivering me from my hardest addiction, and she was finally out of my life! I wanted a partner, not a project, and I was burnt out and had to rise like a Phoenix from these smoldering ashes, and God provided the way! After all, the toughest climbs will lead me to see the greatest view!

Towards the end of this year, a Para-Transit bus driver informed me of a possible job opening at the local *VA hospital*, and I thought this would be an immense highlight on my resume. The position was not available yet, so I started praying for it to be vacant. My normal routine was playing conundrum video games for mental strength, often visiting doctors for my physical well-being, walking miles for endurance and attending church for spiritual growth and understanding. A combination of activities needed to keep me focused on what was next, and as all of this was occurring, Dad and I built our relationship on hope, trust, and humility. We started to understand each other because of the renewing of our minds, and it's gratifying to say that my father went from being my *"most feared"* to my absolute best friend, and now Pop and I can talk comfortably for hours without a hostile vibe in the air. I love Mom and have no conflict with her despite our past disagreements, and there were plenty of them, but she loves me and always provided for me and wants to see me succeed, and as long as I'm aware of this, I can walk well with her. Michael knows most of my likes and could recommend any video game to play, movie to watch or show to view, and I know his input wouldn't leave me disappointed! Desiree and I often disagree on many subjects and respond differently in plenty of areas, and although we may not understand why we are so opposite, maybe if I chose not to act like how I treated her, I could find some common interest, but this is a two-way street. I tip my hat for the future with my family in our rise in unity because I do love them and am very grateful to have no personal issues with any of my family members like I did in my past, and for this, I am blessed!

Around this time, Armando and Jaclyn were dating, and he and I grew close like brothers, and it was great to see the new him, just like I saw a new being within Pops. They were both out with the old and in with the new! Armando and I hung out two or three times a week for months, and it was great playing video games and hanging out with his children. I told him about my faith and asked him to tag along with me to church one day. I attended church with my parents every weekend and even joined the choir because if I wanted to see a change, I needed to make a change! I started becoming a firm believer in my faith. With all the proof provided on why it's so important, I felt the Holy Spirit revitalize me and eventually convicted me to be a member of the church and get baptized because where there is hope, there's life!

The membership class was merged with the baptism course, and since I knew very little about biblical knowledge, I was captivated by the light that would blossom in my head when thinking about walking with the Lord by attending this course, so I was all in! I started memorizing scripture and showed people my faith in action with the Holy Spirit assisting because heaven knows that I cannot do this walk alone. Matthew 7:7 says, *"Ask, and it will be given to you; seek, and you will find; knock, and it will be opened to you."* I was asking for many things, and for many of my requests, God didn't respond for a few reasons. James 4:3 states, *"You ask and do not receive, because you ask with wrong motives, so that you may spend it on your pleasures."* God didn't want me focused on my pleasures; He wanted me to first; as explained in Matthew 6:33, *"Seek the kingdom of God above all else and live righteously, and He will give you everything you need."* I've gambled on many things in my life, but when my soul is literally on the line, it's not wise to play with fire, so it only made sense to now trust who Jesus says He is and watch the miracles form as my faith increases through all circumstances.

There is nothing to lose and much to gain, and if God answers your prayers, the result should increase your faith, and if He delays, He is testing your patience, but if God doesn't answer, He has something better lined up! I saw that I needed to not doubt but rather have *"hope"* as the replacement for uncertainty to experience the abundant life that God promises. Joe as a spiritual leader, said this during bible study, and I wanted to know more. I'm still trying to balance my wants with my necessities, and God knows my best needs.

I was baptized on Easter Sunday! Andrew, Armando, and Jaclyn were in attendance, which was a big deal, and now I could explain to my friends, family and church congregation what God did for me! I never imagined that I would entangle myself with a lot of foolish idiocy, but God had a strong plan for me since my birth and this is only the beginning of my journey. I am certain of Who I can trust, and God has been waiting for this moment for a very long time and let me just say, *I Didn't See That Coming... But He Did!*

CHAPTER 12

MY TESTIMONY: LOST & FOUND FAITH

As many of you may or may not be aware, I lost my eyesight in October of 2009 due to my diabetes. Before I went legally blind, I was about my accomplishments, my skills & my success. I was determined to elevate myself where others had doubts about my abilities. I was continuously in management positions, always had a vehicle, and continually engaged in relationships. It was all about me, but God had other plans lined up for my life. Proverbs 16:9 says, *"The mind of man plans his way, But the Lord directs his steps."* When I lost my ability to see, I can tell you that I've hit rock bottom at this point in my life, and you don't realize how much you love something until it's gone! I'm only thinking about three things at this moment; I can't drive, can't work, and what woman would want me now? I found myself in darkness!

It wasn't easy, but within the first two weeks, my retina was reattached in my left eye, and much transpired during that time. Months after the operation, I would bind myself into a relationship which was foolish since I should have been focusing on concepts bigger than engaging in any rapport. Unfortunately, about two years later, my life started to spiral, which saturated me with rage since my eyesight was getting worse, the relationship I invested in was chaotic, and I needed God's mercy, grace, and the love of Jesus to rescue me. I was now on a productive mission, and it was clear to me that I needed to make Jesus the Lord of my life. God had His perfect plan in arrangement since day one, and it was I who had to be patient and wait to hear Him, for He was calling my name before my birth to listen and follow. *"For I am confident of this very thing, that He who began a good work in you will perfect it until the day of Christ Jesus."* (Philippians 1:6)

In Matthew 5:28-30, Jesus says, "But I tell you, everyone who looks at a woman to lust for her has already committed adultery with her in his heart. If your right eye causes you to sin, gouge it out and throw it away. For it is better that you lose one of the parts of your body than for your whole body to be thrown into hell." Ha-ha, I guess I see why my right eye is gone! Scripture provided me with many reasons not to be concerned. In fact, James

1:2 says, "Consider it all joy, my brethren, when you encounter various trials, knowing that the testing of your faith produces endurance." I started realizing that the bigger picture was not about me. Through the darkness due to my lack of sight, I was grateful & humble to have discovered God's light, and Jesus is the one who shattered the darkness & guided my path! I concluded that He knew me since before my birth, and now it was time for me to know Him on a personal level as opposed to just knowing of Him. After all, it's not what you know but who you know. 2 Corinthians 5:7 says, "We walk by faith, not by sight," and I can proudly say that God made me very familiar with this verse based on His plan for me. 1 Corinthians 15:33 says, "Bad Company Corrupts Good Morals," so with that said, I left the relationship I was in for a better one, one worth having! It's not what I saw but how I saw it that made the difference.

I trusted the death of Jesus Christ on the cross to be my full & ONLY payment for my sins and asked for Him to take the wheel! Will you? I stand in front of you over four years since the loss of my ability to see with an optimistic attitude because I freely think about those three thoughts which used to cloud my judgement. Can I drive? I have a drive, to reach heaven. It may be long distance, but I don't need a car to get there! Can I work? I work for Jesus, and His treasures in heaven are more valuable than anything that this earth can offer me. What woman would want me now? Well, God is my provider, and He will lead the one meant for me toward my direction and make it noticeable. If I could have so much love for the wrong people of my past, I can only imagine how much greater my love would be for the right woman of my future if I'm blessed to receive one! I do know that my relationship with Jesus is forever & what a great relationship it is to inherit. It's great to know that my Lord won't leave me nor forsake me. He is a living, loving, and forgiving God. Those who leave everything in God's hands will eventually see God's hands in everything!

1 John 4:19 says, *"We love because He first loved us."* All I can say is, *"Thank you, Father God, for I no longer look at what I've lost but what I have gained, and it's an honor to accept your will."* When people pass away, there's usually a will of some sort. Who wouldn't want to be a part of God's will? The same God who conquered death! It's great to know that everybody has the ability to be on the winning team of this league. My heavenly Father granted me vision when I needed it, and His Son Jesus provided me strength when I was weak! It's when my eyes stopped looking that my heart found what it needed as opposed to what it wanted, and now, I have Jesus as my Lord and Savior, which means I have eternal life in the Kingdom of God. The only *"I"* that I'm focused on is The Great *"I Am."* Now I can see my accomplishments and my skills, and with Jesus with me, what an amazing success! Put on God's armor, defend yourself with His shield and carry the sword which is His word! Ephesians

6:10-13 states, *"Finally, be strong in the Lord and in the strength of His might. Put on the full armor of God, so that you will be able to stand firm against the schemes of the devil. For our struggle is not against flesh and blood, but against the rulers, against the powers, against the world forces of this darkness, against the spiritual forces of wickedness in the Heavenly places. Therefore, take up the full armor of God, so that you will be able to resist in the evil day, and having done everything, to stand firm."*

My whole life was about seeing a vision, and I was blind prior to the loss of my physical eyesight. I was no longer lost when I found my GPS. After all, to me, G.P.S. stands for *"God Points to Salvation."* Now I'm sure some of you are thinking, *"Well, that's GPtS,"* and yes, it is, but it's that *"t"* that's my reminder of what Christ did for me on the cross. He is God in the flesh! We all go through struggles in our lives, and some are more challenging than others. When you think you have it bad, remember that someone is going through something more challenging! 1 Peter 5:7 states, *"Cast all your anxiety on Him because He cares for you."* Keep in mind the past is history, the future is a mystery, and today is a gift! That's why it's called the *"present"* time. If I dread about my past and worry about my future, I'll miss out on my present time! Matthew 6:34 says, *"So do not worry about tomorrow; for tomorrow will care for itself. Each day has enough trouble of its own."* Jeremiah 29:11-12 says, *"For I know the plans that I have for you; declares the Lord, plans for welfare and not for calamity (disaster) to give you a future and a hope. Then you will call upon Me and come and pray to Me, and I will listen to you."* God listens, so get spiritually adopted and join the family that has already won the war! We are all a soul with a temporary body so take flight with Jesus and accept the gift from God & know that with Jesus Christ as your Lord and Savior, *NOTHING IS IMPOSSIBLE!*

CHAPTER 13

FINAL WORDS

Weeks after I was baptized, I was called in for that interview at the *VA Hospital*, which Armando transported me to, and later that evening, I attended a *"Men's Retreat"* with the guys from church, and about fifty of them were praying over me for God to provide this employment opportunity. Weeks later, I was told that the position in the *Operator's Booth* was now mine! All I had to do was believe and have hope, and since James 5:16 states, *"the effective prayer of a righteous man can accomplish much,"* & Romans 12:12 says, *"Rejoicing in hope, persevering in tribulation, devoted to prayer,"* I knew what needed to be done. I mean, I was not built to task these trials alone, and I thank God that He sent His Son to take the torment that I should have received in hell and placed it upon Himself. I'm saved by grace and not because of my own effort or work. The Lord's Spirit resides within me because I accepted it, and it's that simple, however, it's not easy for some to accept! The hardest walks lead to the greatest destinations! Pray for God to reveal Himself to you because for some, the response is quick, and for others, He is teaching them patience, but either way, He will always respond whether you like the reply or dislike it!

I've expressed my life and who I am, so the question now is, *"Who are you?"* I am a Child of God, a Man of Faith, and a Warrior for Christ, but I will fail every day because I'm perfectly imperfect! My story was filled with bad choices and regret, but everything I have been through brought me toward the path of redemption. I have learned from my mistakes and have risen from the ashes. God wrote this life for me, and my life shall continue with ups and downs until the day my lungs draw their final breath! I will continue to make mistakes, but I'm learning through my process what works and what doesn't. When a difficult situation develops, I try to replace <u>*"Why is this happening to me?"*</u> with <u>*"What is God trying to tell me?"*</u> and I have built discipline in many aspects by trusting Him and being patient! We all have a past, a present, and a future! When it comes to humanity, we are loved when we are born, missed when we die, and in between, we must manage and never forget that God loves us as no human could possibly ever. God didn't save us so we could be bound to our past, He saved us so we could represent Him. I've been protected, directed, and corrected! Protected while encountering all

I was supposed to witness, good and bad, directed from darkness to light and corrected to what God has called for my life.

I was lost and found faith! Moments in life are created with good and bad events; a part of life is the ending! If you can forgive the person, you were, accept the person you are, and believe in the person you will become, you're headed in the right direction! Pops and I dreaded our past, and my Father in Heaven not only transformed my family, but He also enabled my dad to be my greatest comrade! What could my parents do to improve themselves in such a way that they inspired me to be a healthier level of function? Nothing! That was the job of the Holy Spirit, which was the change we all needed, and I witnessed the transformation in all of us! My family and I left Satan's battlefield when we accepted Jesus Christ, and we knew what was worth fighting for and I was willing to listen. No matter what troubles I may encounter, I know my entire family will fight by my side, thick or thin! In the beginning of my story, it appeared that my family did have a problem, but it wasn't a solo Steven issue, and it is defined as sin. The Holy Spirit cleansed all of us for His purpose! Let God write your story and remember to never be a prisoner of your past experiences because it was a life lesson, not a life sentence! God Bless You!!!

ABOUT THE AUTHOR

Steven G. Casado resides in *Westchester County* and lives to try and inspire people with his personal stories and continues striving to be a light on the dark days to those who seek it. He continues inviting people to church for a better understanding of the gospel and enjoys a deep connection in conversation with those willing to engage in it. Steven continues waiting for the right woman to appear in his life, but until then, he remains taking each day as they are provided to him. Steven enjoys long walks, likes traveling, appreciates a good audio descriptive movie and is still a gamer, and has found a balance. However, In December 2018, Steven underwent surgery that was supposed to be a simple procedure when something went terribly wrong. A collapsed lung positioned him into a medically induced coma after being told that he needed his appendix to be removed! Steven refused to lay down his arm to death while being on life support, and although he stared death in the face, God was in control during this spiritual nightmare that Steven experienced. Be on the lookout for that story because if it's God's will, it will be written!